Pescatarian Diet Plan and Cookbook

Your Complete Guide to the Pescatarian Diet. Includes 75+ Delicious Dinner Recipes from All Over the World and a 7-Day Meal Plan

Nancy Peterson

TABLE OF CONTENT

Introduction

A pescatarian is anyone who includes seafood and fish to the vegetarian diet. Different people, for several reasons, may decide to eliminate poultry and meat from their diet but still retain fish. Some vegetarians include fish to their food as they want to not only enjoy the benefits of a plant-based diet but also have a healthy heart. Some others may do this because it suits their taste. While the rest may stick to the pescatarian diet simply because of its impact on the environment.

In this book, we will look at what the pescatarian diet is all about, benefits of this diet, foods to eat and foods not to eat as well as a shopping list to help you succeed with the pescatarian diet. You will also enjoy delicious and easy to make dinner recipes as well as a 7-day meal plan for easy planning of your meals.

Who is a Pescatarian

A pescatarian is someone that includes fish to their diet but avoids meat and other poultry. The term was coined in the early 1990s with a combination of two words, 'Pesce,' which means fish and 'vegetarian.' In summary, a pescatarian is anyone who follows the vegetarian diet, but also includes fish and other seafood to his or her diet. The diet is mainly made up of plant-based foods like legumes, healthy fats, nuts, whole grains, and produce with seafood being the major source of protein.

It may interest you to know that several pescatarians eat eggs and dairy too. In the same way that we have several versions of the vegetarian diet, we also have several versions of the pescatarian diet. One can eat a diet free of meat but packed with plenty of junk foods, processed starches, and fish sticks instead of a healthier diet made up of whole foods.

Reasons to Follow a Pescatarian Diet

Several people follow the pescatarian diet for different reasons. Some of these reasons are:

1.   **Health benefits**

Research has proven that plant-based diets have several advantages, including lowering the risk of obesity and chronic diseases like diabetes and heart disease. Research also shows that you can get these protective benefits from following the pescatarian diet.

One study proved that women who followed the pescatarian diet gained 2.5 fewer pounds than women who had meat included in their diet. Also, people who changed their diet to plant-based gained the least amount of weight. This means that reducing your consumption of meat and poultry may be beneficial to your health regardless of your current eating patterns.

Another study concluded that people on a pescatarian diet had reduced the risk of developing diabetes at 4.8 percent compared to omnivores at 7.6 percent.

Also, one study looked at people who were pescatarian or rarely ate meat, and it discovered that these people had a 22 percent lower risk of dying from heart diseases when compared to people who eat meat regularly.

2. Environmental concerns

United Nations quoted that raising livestock contributes to 15 percent of all human-made carbon emissions. While producing fish and other seafood generates lower carbon than any animal meat or cheese.

One study conducted in 2014 calculated that fish eaters' diets caused 46 percent less greenhouse gas emissions than that of people who consumed at least one serving of meat each day.

3. Ethical reasons

Some people may choose to be vegetarians for ethical reasons, and the same applies to pescatarians. Some ethical reasons for which people may prefer to avoid meat in their diet include:

- **Inhumane factory practices:** they are not in support of factory farms that raise livestock in harsh and inhumane conditions.
- **Opposing slaughter:** they do not support the killing of animals for food.
- **Humanitarian reasons:** they believe producing grain to feed to animals is a waste of resources and land, considering the level of hunger in the world.
- **Poor labor conditions:** they do not want to be a part of factory farms that treat their workers poorly.

What do Pescatarians Eat?

- Peanuts and seeds, nuts and nut butter
- Whole grains and grain products
- Vegetables
- Fruits
- Seeds including flaxseeds, chia, and hemp
- Legumes including lentils, hummus, tofu and beans

- Dairy including cheese, milk, and yogurt

- Shellfish and fish

- Eggs

What not to Eat

- Pork

- Turkey

- Chicken

- Beef

- Lamb

- Wild game

Benefits of Adding Fish to a Vegetarian Diet

You will enjoy several benefits when you add fish to the vegetarian diet. Several people are worried that avoiding animal flesh or totally eliminating animal products could cause a low intake of certain vital nutrients. For instance, it is tough to get protein, calcium, zinc, and vitamin B12 on a vegan diet. When you add seafood like mollusks, crustaceans, and fish to the vegetarian diet, you will begin to enjoy vital nutrients and varieties in your diet.

- **Get more omega-3s**

The best way to get omega-3 fatty acids is by consuming fish. Some plant-based foods like flaxseed walnuts contain alpha-linolenic acid, which is a type of omega-3 fat. But it is not easy for the body to convert this type of acid to **docosahexaenoic acid DHA** and eicosapentaenoic acid (EPA). EPA and DHA have more benefits that are helpful to the heart, brain, and mood. Oily fish like sardines and salmon contain both DHA and EPA.

- **Boost your protein intake**

Every person needs a daily intake of about 0.8g of protein per 2.2 pounds of body weight to stay healthy. So, a person who weighs 150 pounds needs to eat a minimum of 54 grams of protein daily. It can be tough to achieve a high protein diet with just plant-based foods, particularly if you do not want extra fat or carbs with your protein. An excellent source of lean protein is fish and other seafood, as it gives your body the protein needed for the body to perform optimally.

- **Seafood has other nutrients**

Apart from protein and omega-3s, seafood is rich in several other nutrients. For example, oysters have a high content of vitamin B12, selenium, and zinc. One oyster gives 55 percent of the RDI for selenium and zinc, as well as 133 percent of the RDI for vitamin B12.

Mussel is another seafood that has high contents of selenium, manganese, vitamin B12, and other B vitamins. White fish varieties like flounder and cod do not have much omega-3 fats but provide extremely lean protein. For instance, 3 ounces of cod produces less than a gram of fat and 19 grams of protein. Cod is a great choice for people who need niacin, phosphorus, selenium, vitamins B6 and vitamins B12

- **Gives you more options**

The vegetarian diet can be limiting at times, especially when eating out at restaurants. If you eat food to stay healthy, then being a pescatarian offers you more meal options. And fish makes a good option as you can prepare it in several ways; grill, bake or sautee.

7-Day Pescatarian Diet Meal Plan

People who are just beginning the pescatarian diet may find it difficult to design their meals for the next few weeks. This may cause some people to default to eating more of high carb meals, which is not the best way to maintain a healthy balanced diet. One of the great benefits of this diet is that you get to enjoy plenty of omega-3 fatty acids from fish, which will lower inflammation in the body.

So, let's get started with the seven days meal plan to guide you in designing yours.

DAY 1

Breakfast

- Avocado Baked Eggs

Lunch

- Moroccan Stuffed Sweet Potato skins

Dinner

- Thai Massaman Curry

DAY 2

Breakfast

- Spanish egg muffins

Lunch

- Mac n cheese

Dinner

- Baked tilapia with a parmesan crust

Dinner (side)

- Bowl of rice

DAY 3

9

Breakfast

- Huevos Rancheros

Snack

- Chocolate peanut butter protein ball

Lunch

- Mackerel and green bean salad

Dinner

- Teriyaki stir fry

DAY 4

Breakfast

- Avocado and sautéed mushroom toast

Lunch

- Greek chickpea salad

Dinner

- Vegan red lentil curry

Dinner (side)

- Coriander and garlic naan

DAY 5

Breakfast

- Fresh Sardine Fillets on toast

Snack

- Vegan protein balls

Lunch

- Aloo Gobi with chickpeas

Dinner

- Roasted tomato soup

Dinner Side

- 2x slices of bread

DAY 6

Breakfast

- Smoked salmon egg muffins

Snack

- Vegan protein balls

Lunch

- Curried butternut squash soup

Dinner

- Tuna pesto pasta

DAY 7

Breakfast

- Blueberry and lemon muffins

Lunch

- Udon noodle soup

Dinner

- Swett and sticky salmon kebabs

Dinner Side

- Carrot hummus cucumber cups

7-Day Meal Plan Recipes (Breakfast, Lunch, Dinner, Snacks, and Side)

Day 1

Breakfast: Avocado Baked Eggs

Prep Time: 3 minutes

Cook Time: 15 minutes

Total Time: 18 minutes

Serves: 1 person

Ingredients

- Eggs – 2
- Avocado – 1
- Pinch of black pepper
- Juice of ¼ lemon
- A handful of cilantro (chopped)

Instructions

- Preheat your oven to 425 degrees Fahrenheit.
- Use a sharp knife to cut the avocado in half, then use a spoon or your hands to remove the seed.

- Scoop out a slightly large amount of avocado to create space to fit in your eggs. You can quickly achieve this using a teaspoon.

- Squeeze the juice of the lemon on top of each of the avocado halves to prevent them from turning brown in the oven. Then break your eggs into each half of the avocado, and sprinkle a pinch of pepper and salt on top of the halves.

- Place them inside a muffin tin or on a small baking tray and place in the oven to bake for approx. 15 minutes.

- Take out of the oven, allow to stand for 1 minute before serving.

Lunch: Moroccan Stuffed Sweet Potato skins

Prep Time: 5 minutes

Cook Time: 1 hour

Total Time: 1 hour, 5 minutes

Serves: 4 stuffed sweet potatoes

Ingredients

- Chickpeas – 1 can (drained)
- Sweet potatoes – 2
- Cumin – 2 tsp
- Garlic – 2 cloves (finely chopped)
- Ground coriander – 1 tsp
- Black pepper ½ tsp
- Parsley – 1 handful (finely chopped)
- Paprika – 1 tsp
- Salt – 1 tsp
- Feta cheese - 40g, cut into cubes

Instructions

- Preheat your oven to 370 degrees F.
- Use your knife to cut a few shallow slits in the potatoes before you place them into a baking tray, then place into the oven to roast for about 40 mins.
- While the potatoes are in the oven, add the parsley, paprika, coriander, chickpeas, cumin, and garlic to a large bowl and mix thoroughly.
- Take out the potatoes from the oven and cut horizontally in half. Use your spoon to scoop out

the sweet potatoes, ensuring to leave about 2cm of the potatoes attached to the skin.

- Chop the potatoes into bite-size pieces and mix with the chickpeas so that they are well coated with the spices.

- Spoon back the contents of the bowl into the sweet potato skins. Add the feta cubes and return to the oven to bake for another 15 minutes.

- Take out of the oven and serve hot.

Dinner: Thai Vegetable Massaman Curry

Prep Time: 10 minutes

Cook Time: 30 minutes

Total Time: 40 minutes

Serves: 3 people

Ingredients

For Curry Paste

- Fresh ginger – 1 tsp

- Red Chili – 1 (finely chopped)

- Galangal – 1 tsp

- Green Chili – 1 (finely chopped)
- Coriander seeds – 1 tsp
- Garlic – 2 cloves (finely chopped)
- Fresh ginger – 1 tsp
- Fresh coriander - 30g (finely chopped)
- Turmeric – 1 tbsp
- Ground nutmeg – 1 tsp
- Ground cumin - 1 tbsp
- Fish sauce - 10ml
- Vegetable oil - 10ml
- Soy sauce - 10ml

For Curry

- Large bay leaf – 1
- Coconut milk - 400ml
- Coconut cream - 160ml
- White potatoes - 200g (peel and cut into bite-size pieces)
- Cashew nuts - 50g
- Shallots - 3 (cut into quarters)

Instructions

- position a large wok over high heat and add turmeric, coriander seeds, ground cumin, and nutmeg to the wok once heated up. Ensure to grind the coriander seeds using a mortar and pestle before adding to the pot. The pot also needs to be dry when adding these ingredients as you are only dry roasting the powders to give the needed flavor. This will take about 30 seconds, and the minute you begin to stir the content, you will begin to perceive the aroma.

- Now add the fresh coriander, galangal, fish sauce, soy, ginger, garlic, Chilies, and vegetable oil to the wok. Stir the pan occasionally for 30 seconds until you have a wet paste.

- Now add the cashew nuts, potatoes, and shallots, stir together until lightly coated.

- Add the bay leaf, coconut milk, and coconut cream. Mix everything together. Allow the pan to boil, then lower the heat to simmer. Allow the curry to simmer for about 25 to 30 minutes, then remove the bay leaf and serve!

DAY 2

Breakfast: Spanish Style Egg Muffins

Prep Time: 20 minutes

Cook Time: 15 minutes

Total Time: 35 minutes

Serves: 6 egg muffins

Ingredients

- Large eggs - 6
- shallot – 1 (finely chopped)
- Green pepper – ¼ (finely chopped)
- Garlic – 1 clove (finely chopped)
- Red pepper – ¼ (finely chopped)
- Paprika – ½ tsp
- Tomatoes – 60g
- Glug of olive oil

Instructions

- Preheat your oven to 390 degrees F
- On medium heat, place a small frypan and add the olive oil.

- Once the oil gets hot, add the leave and the shallot to sweat with the lid on for approx. 3 minutes.

- Now add the tomatoes, peppers, paprika, and garlic and cook for another 5 minutes. Stir occasionally, so they do not stick. Take off heat and keep the pan aside to cool.

- Break and beat your eggs in a large bowl or jug. Then add the contents of your frypan to the bowl, season with pepper and salt.

- Spoon the ingredients into muffin tray and place in the oven to bake for about 15 minutes, until the muffins are springy and fluffy.

- Take out of the oven and serve!

Lunch: Mac and Cheese with Spinach and Cauliflower

Prep Time: 25 minutes

Cook Time: 40 minutes

Total Time: 1 hour, 5 minutes

Serves: 4 people

Ingredients

- Macaroni pasta - 220g

- Garlic – 3 cloves (minced)

- Butter - 30g

- Flour - 2 tbsp

- Milk - 325ml

- Paprika - ½ tsp

- Cauliflower head -2/3 (cut into bite-size florets)

- Spinach - 40g

- Cheddar - 100g (grated)

- Parmesan - 30g (grated)

- Handful of breadcrumbs

Instructions

- Preheat your oven to 360 degrees F.

- Boil the macaroni according to the instruction on the pack. Once cooked, drain the liquid and keep aside.

- Place a large saucepan over low heat, add your butter, then add the minced garlic and cook for a few minutes.

- Now add your flour, one tablespoon at a time. Use a wooden spoon to mix with the butter.

- Then slowly add the milk while whisking to ensure the sauce is lump-free and smooth.

- Take the saucepan off the heat and slowly stir in most of the parmesan and cheddar, reserve a small handful of each to sprinkle over your dish.

- Stir in the spinach, cauliflower, paprika, and macaroni, mix to get them coated with the cheese sauce. It may seem like the spinach is a lot at first, but you will notice that it will begin to wilt down.

- Now pour the mixture into an oven-proof dish and sprinkle your parmesan, cheddar, and breadcrumbs on top.

- Place the dish into the oven to bake for about 30 to 40 minutes until the top is crispy and golden.

Dinner: Baked Tilapia with Parmesan Crust

Prep Time: 15 minutes

Cook Time: 20 minutes

Total Time: 35 minutes

Serves: 2 people

Ingredients

- Tilapia – 2 fillets
- Vegetarian parmesan - 100g (finely grated)
- Breadcrumbs - 40g
- Parsley – a handful (finely chopped)
- Paprika - 1.5 tsp
- Black pepper - ½ tsp
- Olive oil - 3 tbsp
- Lemon – 1 (cut into wedges)

Instructions

- Preheat your oven to 400 degrees F.
- Mix the breadcrumbs, parsley, black pepper, paprika, and grated Parmesan in a bowl. Spread the mixture across a big, flat baking tray and keep aside.
- Mix the olive oil and lemon in a small bowl. Rub the olive oil mixture all over the tilapia fillet, leaving just a little oil. Then dip the oiled fillets into the parmesan mixture, ensure to cover the whole fillet.
- Check through the fillets for any side not properly covered and dab the leftover oil on it before sprinkling the parmesan mix.

- Place the tilapia fillets in the oven and allow to bake for about 20 minutes, until the fish is white and flaky and the crust turns golden.

DAY 3

Breakfast: Huevos Rancheros

Prep Time: 5 minutes

Cook Time: 20 minutes

Total Time: 25 minutes

Serves: 4 people

Ingredients

- Orange pepper – ½ (slice into strips)
- Red pepper – ½ (slice into strips)
- Vine tomatoes - 4 (quartered)
- Onion – 1 (diced)
- Garlic - 1 clove (finely chopped)
- Smoked paprika - 1 tsp
- Free-range eggs – 4
- Vegetable or rapeseed oil - 1 tbsp
- Pinto beans - 50g

- Kidney beans - 50g
- Chopped tomatoes - 1 tin

Instructions

- Position a deep frypan on high heat, then add the rapeseed oil. You can use vegetable oil in place of rapeseed oil.
- Now add the garlic, vine tomatoes, and onion to the pan and fry for approx five minutes while stirring occasionally.
- Once the onion is soft, add the pinto beans, peppers, kidney beans, and butter beans. Pour the tin of tomatoes then add a pinch of sugar to remove the tartness. Now add the smoked paprika, season with pepper and salt, then mix the contents of the pan. Lower the heat to medium and leave to simmer for approx. fifteen minutes, stirring frequently.
- Use the back of a large serving spoon to make four small wells in the mixture then break an egg into each well. Reduce the heat to low and cook for another 3 to 4 minutes or until the egg whites turn white.

- Take the pan off the heat once you achieve this and allow it to stand for a few minutes.

- Serve with some flatbread.

Snack: Chocolate Peanut Butter Protein Ball

Prep Time: 10 minutes

Total Time: 10 minutes

Serves: 12 protein balls

Ingredients

- Rolled oats - 2 cups (170g)

- Cocoa powder - 2 tsp

- Protein powder - 4 tbsp

- Nutmeg - 1 tsp

- Sesame seeds - 2 tbsp

- Semi-sweet chocolate chips - 1/3 (50g) cup (60% cocoa)

- Peanut butter - 4 tbsp

- Vanilla extract - 1 tsp

- Honey - 2 tbsp

Instructions

- Add the cocoa powder, rolled oats, sesame seeds, nutmeg, protein powder, chocolate chips, vanilla extract honey and peanut butter to a large bowl. Stir together until the contents combine properly.

- Now use your hand to shape the mixture into balls by rolling between your palms. Add a couple drops of water if the mixture seems too dry.

- You should get 12 even shaped balls. Place each ball on a baking tray and keep in the fridge for a minimum of 30 minutes to firm up.

Lunch: Green Bean and Mackerel Salad

Prep Time: 12 minutes

Cook Time: 6 minutes

Total Time: 18 minutes

Serves: 2 people

Ingredients

- Large free-range eggs - 4

- Sugar snap peas - 90g

- Garden peas - 50g

- Green beans - 100g

- Avocado – 1 (peel and cut into cubes)

- Spring mixed salad leaves - 60g
- Mackerel - 50g
- Black pepper - 1 tsp
- Juice of 1/4 lemon

Ingredients

- Add water to a saucepan over medium heat, add the eggs once the water begins to boil and leave for about 3 minutes. Now add the green beans and sugar snap peas and cook for another 3 minutes.
- Take out the eggs from the pot and briefly run under cold water. Drain the sugar snap peas and green beans.
- Add the avocado mackerel, garden peas, lemon juice, green beans, salad leaves, and the sugar snap peas into a large salad bowl. Mix thoroughly.
- Peel the eggs, then quarter them open over the salad, so that the egg yolk runs over the salad, add the egg white to the salad. Serve.

Dinner: Teriyaki stir fry

Prep Time: 9 minutes

Cook Time: 11 minutes

Total Time: 20 minutes

Serves: 2 people

Ingredients

- Teriyaki sauce - 4 tbsp
- Sesame oil - 1 tbsp
- Green chili pepper – ½ (finely chopped)
- Onion – ½ (finely chopped)
- Mushroom - 50g (finely sliced)
- Ginger – a thumb (finely chopped)
- Garlic - 2 cloves (finely chopped)
- Red bell pepper – ½ (roughly chopped)
- Green bell pepper– ½ (roughly chopped)
- Celery – 2 stalks (roughly chopped)
- Carrots – 3 (peel and cut into thin slices)
- Broccoli head – 1 (cut into florets)
- Sesame seeds - 20g
- Green beans - 45g
- Soy sauce - 1 tbsp
- A handful of cashew nuts
- Juice of 1/2 a lime

Instructions

- Place a wok on high heat, then add the sesame oil. Add the garlic, onion, chili, and ginger, once the oil is hot, and fry for about 3 minutes.

- Then add the cashew nuts and the remaining vegetables and fry for another 7 to 8 minutes, until the veggies are softened a little, and the colors are out.

- Add the soy sauce, lime, and teriyaki sauce and mix to coat the veggies. Sprinkle in the sesame seeds and fry for another 1 minute.

- Take wok away from heat and serve.

DAY 4

Breakfast: Avocado and Sautéed Mushroom Toast

Prep Time: 5 minutes

Cook Time: 3 minutes

Total Time: 8 minutes

Serves: 1 person

Ingredients

- Mushrooms - 150g

- Avocado – 1 (chop into segments)

- Olive oil - 2 tbsp

- Sourdough bread - 2 slices
- Pinch of pepper
- Pinch of salt

Instructions

- Heat the olive oil in a frypan over medium-high heat.
- Place the bread in the grill or a toaster and leave for about 2 to 3 minutes, until brown.
- Add the mushrooms to the frypan as well as a pinch of black pepper and salt. Fry for 3 minutes until they begin to lightly brown.
- Spread the slices of avocado over your toast bread. Then pour the mushrooms as well as any remaining olive oil.
- Enjoy!

Lunch: Greek chickpea salad

Prep Time: 10 minutes

Total Time: 10 minutes

Serves: 2 people

Ingredients

- grape tomatoes - 100g (quartered)
- Chickpeas - 1 can (drained)

- Garlic - 3 cloves (minced)

- green chili - ½ (deseed and finely chop)

- scallions – 5 (chop into small discs)

- feta - 30g (cut into cubes)

For the dressing

- Juice of 1/4 lemon

- Black pepper – ½ tsp

- Olive oil - 1 tbsp

Instructions

- Add all the salad ingredients into a large bowl and mix thoroughly.

- Add all the dressing ingredients to another bowl or jug and whisk together, then drizzle over the salad.

- If not using all of the dressing, place in an airtight container and put in the fridge for up to one week.

Dinner: Vegan red lentil curry

Prep Time: 10 minutes

Cook Time: 25 minutes

Total Time: 35 minutes

Serves: 4 people

Ingredients

- Sesame oil - 2 tbsp
- Garlic - 3 cloves (finely chopped)
- Ginger - 1 thumb (finely chopped)
- Red chili pepper – ½ (finely chopped)
- White scallions – 5 (finely chopped)
- Curry powder - 2 tbsp
- Celery – 1 stalk (roughly chopped)
- Cumin - 1 tsp
- Chili powder - 1 tsp
- Tomato paste – 1 tbsp
- Vegetable stock - 3 cups
- Carrots – 3 (cut into discs)
- Red lentils - 1 cup
- A handful of spinach leaves
- Pinch of pepper and salt
- A handful of cilantro, finely chopped
- Juice of ¼ lime

Instructions

- Place a large saucepan over medium heat and pour the sesame oil. Now add the chili pepper, garlic, ginger, celery, and scallions.

Fry for about 5 minutes, until the vegetables are slightly softened.

- Then add the tomato paste, chili powder, lentils, cumin, curry powder, carrots, then stir together to get all the veggies coated in the spices. Pour the vegetable stock and allow to boil, then reduce heat and simmer for approx. 15 minutes.

- Finally, squeeze in the lime juice to the saucepan, add the spinach leaves, and seasoning for taste. Stir. Garnish with the chopped cilantro.

- Serve!

Dinner (Side): Coriander and Garlic Naan

Prep Time: 1 hour, 20 minutes

Cook Time: 10 minutes

Total Time: 1 hour, 30 minutes

Serves: 4 naan bread

Ingredients

- All-purpose flour - 2 cups

- Sugar - 1 tsp

- Yeast - 1 tsp

- Warm water – 5 ½ fl oz
- Butter - 1 tbsp

For the garlic cilantro butter

- Melted butter, unsalted - 4 tablespoons
- A handful of cilantro, finely chopped
- Garlic - 2 cloves (minced)

Instructions

- Pour the warm water into a jug, add sugar and yeast. Stir well and keep aside for some minutes.

- Get a large bowl, sieve in the flour, add salt, and use your spoon to create a well in the middle, then add 1 tbsp of butter, and the yeast mixture then stir together with a wooden spoon. Once combined, place dough on a lightly floured surface and knead for about 5 minutes until the dough becomes slightly elastic and smooth. Peradventure the dough sticks to your hand, simply add a little more dough and knead further.

- Cover the dough with a kitchen towel and keep in a warm area. Leave for one hour to rise.

- Ten minutes before the dough is ready for use, preheat the broiler over high heat.

- Place a small pot over medium heat and melt 2 tbsp butter, then add the cilantro, and minced garlic. Fry for about 2 minutes, then take away the pot from heat and keep aside.

- Lightly flour a work surface, then place the dough on the surface and cut into 4 pieces. Roll out each piece into a circle of approx. 1-inch thick and then place on a greased oven tray.

- Place the naans in the oven to bake for approx. eight minutes, ensure to turn them about 3 to 4 times to stop the bottom of the naan from becoming flat and hard. Whenever you turn the naan, brush with garlic butter mixture from the pot.

- Once the naans are ready, place them on a plate and allow them to cool a little before serving with delicious curry.

DAY 5

Breakfast: Fresh Sardine Fillets on toast

Prep Time: 10 minutes

Cook Time: 5 minutes

Total Time: 15 minutes

Serves: 4 slices of toast (2 people)

Ingredients

- 12 fresh sardine fillets (from 6 sardines, about ½ lb), cleaned and gutted
- Lemon juice - 2 tbsp
- Olive oil - 3 tbsp
- Salt – ½ tsp
- Garlic – 2 cloves (finely chopped)
- Fresh parsley – ½ tbsp (roughly chopped)
- Red Chili pepper – ½ (finely chopped)

Instructions

- Mix 1 tbsp of lemon juice and one tablespoon of olive oil. Then rub the mixture on each of the sardine fillets and sprinkle salt over the fillets.
- Now position a large pot over medium heat and add 1 tbsp of olive oil to the pot. Once

hot, add the chili and garlic and fry for 2 minutes.

- Place the fillets into the hot pot, with the skin side facing down. Cook for about 3 minutes, until the flesh is less translucent and white. At this same time, toast the bread.

- Transfer the toast to your plate and add three sardine fillets on each toast slice. Drizzle the remaining lemon juice and olive oil over the sardines, then sprinkle the parsley on the toast. Serve!

Snack: Vegan Protein Balls

Prep Time: 10 minutes

Total Time: 10 minutes

Serves: 10 protein balls

Ingredients

- Oats - 1 ½ cup

- Vanilla extract - 1 tsp

- Vegan soy protein powder – 2/3 cup

- Cinnamon - 2 tsp

- Sesame seeds - 1 tbsp

- Raisins - 5 tbsp
- Almond milk - ¼ cup

Instructions

- Place the protein powder, sesame seeds, raisins, cinnamon, and oats into a large bowl.
- Add half of the milk and the vanilla extract. Stir thoroughly.
- Now slowly add the remaining almond milk, as much as is needed to get a sticky mixture, so that it can easily be rolled into balls.
- Roll the dough into 12 protein balls using the palms of your hands, then keep in the fridge for about 30 to 40 minutes until they are firm and held together.

Lunch: Aloo Gobi with Chickpeas

Prep Time: 10 minutes

Cook Time: 20 minutes

Total Time: 30 minutes

Serves: 2 people

Ingredients

- Whole cauliflower – 1 (cut into florets)

- Canola oil - 50ml

- Green Chili - ½ (chopped finely)

- Large white potato – 1 (peel and cut into large cubes)

- Garlic - 2 cloves (finely chop)

- Cilantro - 1 handful (finely chopped)

- Chickpeas - ½ can

- Turmeric - 1 tbsp

- Ground coriander - ½ tbsp

- Salt - 1 tsp

- Water - ½ cup

- Black pepper - 1 tsp

Instructions

- Place a deep saute pan over medium-high heat, then add the canola oil.

- Once hot, add the turmeric, green chili, garlic, and ground coriander and fry for about 40 to 50 seconds. This will be the spice paste that you will use to flavor your dish.

- Now add the cauliflower, potato, cilantro and mix thoroughly, until the potatoes and cauliflower turn yellow.

- Then add the chickpeas and water and stir together. Allow the water to boil, then lower the heat, cover the pot and allow to simmer for approx. 15 minutes.
- Transfer content of the pan to a large serving bowl, sprinkle the chopped cilantro on top. Enjoy!

Dinner: Roast Tomato Soup with Garlic Croutons

Prep Time: 10 minutes

Cook Time: 1 hour, 20 minutes

Total Time: 1 hour, 30 minutes

Serves: 4 people

Ingredients

- Garlic - 4 cloves (peeled)
- Large onion – 1 (roughly chopped)
- Overripe tomatoes - 3 ½ lbs (cut into quarters)
- Olive oil - 1 tbsp
- Oregano - 1 tsp
- Cracked black pepper - 1 tsp
- Red wine vinegar - 2 tbsp
- Vegetable stock – 2 ½ cups
- Basil leaves – 5

For the croutons

- Garlic - 3 cloves (minced)
- Stale bread - 2 slices (cut into cubes)
- Unsalted butter - 1 oz

Instructions

- Preheat your oven to 375 degrees F.
- Add the garlic, onions, and tomatoes with the skin down into a large baking tray. Sprinkle black pepper and oregano on top and drizzle the olive oil. Place in the oven to roast for approx. 1 hour.
- Once roasted, place a large saucepan over medium heat, add the basil leaves, vegetable stock, and all the roasted veggies.
- Allow the pot to boil then add the red wine vinegar. Lower the heat and allow to simmer for approx. 5 minutes.
- Now blend the contents of the pan until you have a smooth consistency. Add more seasoning if needed.

To Make the Croutons

- Place a small pot over medium heat and add the butter. Once melted, add the minced garlic and fry for about 2 minutes.

- Add the bread cubes to the saucepan and mix well with the garlic butter.
- Line baking sheet on a baking tray, pour the mixture into the tray and place in the oven to bake for about 10 to 12 minutes, until it turns golden.

Dinner Side

- 2x slices of bread

DAY 6

Breakfast: Smoked Salmon Egg Muffins

Prep Time: 15 minutes

Cook Time: 15 minutes

Total Time: 30 minutes

Serves: 6 egg muffins

Ingredients

- Mushrooms - 70g (finely chopped)
- White onion – ½ (finely chopped)
- Garlic – 1 clove (minced)
- Eggs - 6
- Handful spinach
- smoked salmon - 40g
- Glug of vegetable oil
- Salt and pepper

Instructions

- Preheat your oven to 390 degrees F.
- Place a frypan over medium heat, then pour in the vegetable oil.
- Now add the mushrooms and chopped onions, cook for about 3 minutes, while stirring frequently. Then add the garlic and fry for an additional 2 minutes.
- Put off the heat and keep the frypan aside to cool, along with its content.
- Beat your eggs in a large bowl, then add salt and pepper, the spinach, and the smoked salmons in small sizes.
- Now add all the ingredients of the frypan to the large bowl.
- Mix and pour the mixture into a muffin tray. Place the tray in the oven to bake for approx. 15 minutes and your meal is ready.

Snack

- Vegan protein balls

Lunch: Curried Butternut Squash Soup

Prep Time: 25 minutes

Cook Time: 35 minutes

Total Time: 1 hour

Serves: 4 people

Ingredients

- Butternut squash - 1 (peel and cube)
- Coconut oil - 1 tbsp
- Small onion – 1 (roughly chopped)
- Red Chili – ½ (roughly chopped)
- Vegetable stock - 500ml
- Garlic - 3 cloves (roughly chopped)
- Curry powder - 3 tsp
- Salt - 1 tsp
- Black pepper - 1 tsp
- Nutmeg – ½ tsp
- Coconut milk - 400ml tin
- A handful of coriander, roughly chopped

Serving options

- Coriander - 1 handful (finely chopped)
- Seeds from 1 butternut squash
- Sour cream - 3 tbsp

Instructions

- place a large soup pot over medium-high heat and add the coconut oil. Add the onion once the oil gets hot and fry for about 3 minutes, stirring often. Now add the chili and garlic and cook for another 3 minutes.
- Add the curry powder, coriander, nutmeg, butternut squash, salt, and pepper and stir together to coat the veggies with your seasoning and spices.
- Reduce the heat and add the vegetable stock as well as the coconut milk. Stir quickly and leave for about 15 minutes, until the squash is soft and you can easily pass a knife through it.
- If you want to use the squash seeds to garnish, you will need to toast it in the oven at 350 degrees F. add the seed to the oven once hot and toast for 15 minutes or until the seeds begin to pop.
- Now add the soup to your soup blender and blend until you have a smooth consistency. Taste and adjust seasoning as needed, then keep aside for 5 minutes.
- Serve with your preferred garnish.

Dinner: Tuna and Pesto Pasta

Prep Time: 20 minutes

Cook Time: 10 minutes

Total Time: 30 minutes

Serves: 6 people

Ingredients

- Garlic - 4 cloves
- Fusili Pasta - 600g
- Rocket - 150g
- Parsley - 20g
- Olive oil - 4 tbsp
- Vegetarian parmesan - 20g (grated)
- Pea shoots - 50g
- 200g tins of tuna – 2
- Pinch of black pepper
- One lemon, zest, and juice

Instructions

- Cook the pasta until al dente, following the instruction on the pack.
- Reserve half cup of the pasta liquid for later and drain the remaining liquid.

- Add the garlic cloves, half of the grated Parmesan, lemon zest and juice, the parsley, 3/4 of the rocket, olive oil, and the black pepper into your food processor, blend until you have a good looking pesto. You may have to add the ingredients in batches if you have a small food processor.
- Place a large pot over low heat, add the tuna, the cooked pasta, and the pesto to the pot. Mix until the pesto completely covers the pasta. Feel free to add a little of the pasta water if you have a very thick pesto. Put off heat, add the remaining rocket, and the pea shoots.
- Serve with some grated Parmesan on top!

DAY 7

Breakfast: Blueberry and Lemon Muffins

Prep Time: 15 minutes

Cook Time: 25 minutes

Total Time: 40 minutes

Serves: 12-15 muffins

Ingredients

- Butter - 1 stick (115g)
- Sugar - 1 cup/ 200g
- Blueberries – 1 ½ cups (200g)
- Zest of 1 lemon
- Large eggs – 2
- Milk - 1 cup (250ml)
- Vanilla extract - ½ tsp
- Baking powder - 2 tsp
- Flour – 2 ½ cups (300g)
- Salt - ¼ tsp
- Juice of 1/4 lemon
- Nutmeg - ½ tsp

Instructions

- Preheat your oven to 350 degrees F.
- Place the lemon zest, butter, and sugar in a mixer and beat until fluffy and light.
- Now add the lemon juice, milk, vanilla extract, and milk a little at a time. Beat quickly each time you add a new ingredient.
- Sieve the baking powder, flour, nutmeg, and salt into the mixing bowl and fold into the batter until the flour is well incorporated.

- Finally, stir in the blueberries and spoon the batter into a muffin tray. Place the tray into the oven to bake for approx. 25 minutes until golden brown. To confirm that the muffin is ready, insert a knife into any of the muffins, it should come out clean.

Lunch: Vegetarian Udon Noodle Soup

Prep Time: 8 minutes

Cook Time: 16 minutes

Total Time: 24 minutes

Serves: 4 people

Ingredients

- Celery – 1 stick (finely chopped)
- Sesame oil - 1 tbsp
- Cilantro, finely chopped - 1 handful
- Garlic - 4 cloves (finely chopped)
- Ginger - 1 thumb (finely chopped)
- Green serrano Chili – ½ (finely chopped)
- Large broccoli head – 1 (cut into florets)
- Scallions – 3 (finely chopped)
- Vegetable stock - 6 cups
- Mushrooms - 5.3 oz (sliced thinly)

- Sliced water chestnuts - 1 5oz can

- Soy sauce - 5 tbsp

- Teriyaki sauce - 3 tbsp

- Udon noodles - 6oz

Instructions

- Place a large pot over medium heat and add the sesame oil. Once hot, add the scallions, ginger, garlic, broccoli, celery, and chili and fry for about 3 minutes, stirring occasionally.

- Now add the water chestnuts and mushrooms. Fry for another 2 minutes.

- Add the vegetable stock, the teriyaki sauce, and the soy sauce and bring to a boil. Now reduce the heat and allow to simmer for 10 minutes.

- While simmering, cook the noodles according to the instruction on the packet.

- Once the noodle is done, add them to your soup and serve with the chopped cilantro in each bowl.

Dinner: Sweet and Sticky Salmon Kebabs

Prep Time: 1 hour, 20 minutes

Cook Time: 10 minutes

Total Time: 1 hour, 30 minutes

Serves: 6 kebabs

Ingredients

- Dijon mustard - 1 tsp
- Juice of ½ lemon
- Olive oil - 1 tbsp
- Garlic, minced - 1 clove
- Salmon fillet – 1 (cut into bite-size cubes)
- Red chili flakes - ½ tsp
- Honey - 1 tsp
- Red onion - ½ (cut into bite-size cubes)
- Small tomatoes – 10 (cherry tomatoes or grape are perfect), halved
- Zucchini - ½ (cut into thin discs)
- Lemon - ½ (cut into thin discs)

Instructions

- Mix the olive oil, mustard, minced garlic, honey, lemon juice, and chili flakes in a large bowl. Spoon half of the sauce over the salmon pieces and keep in the fridge for at least one hour, to marinate.
- Five minutes to the expiration of the one hour, preheat the grill to high heat. Chop all your veggies. Then begin to place a piece of salmon

and veggie on a kebab skewer. Repeat until the skewer is filled.

- Now place all the filed kebab skewers on a baking tray and brush the leftover marinade over each kebab.
- Place the skewers in the oven for about 10 minutes, 5 minutes on each side. You can confirm that the kebab is done once the salmon begins to burn a little on the outside.
- Serve with pasta, rice, or quinoa.

Dinner Side: Carrot Hummus Cucumber Cups

Prep Time: 20 minutes

Cook Time: 25 minutes

Total Time: 45 minutes

Serves: 12 cucumber cups (6 people)

Ingredients

- Large cucumbers – 2
- Carrots - 1 lb (peel and cut into small sticks)
- Garlic - 3 cloves (peeled)
- Honey - 1 tsp
- Salt - ½ tsp
- olive oil - 3 tbsp

- Cumin - 1 tsp

- Ground coriander - 1 tsp

- Black pepper - ½ tsp

- Tahini - 3 tbsp

- Lemon juice - 2 tbsp

- Chopped cilantro - 1 handful

Instructions

- Preheat your oven to 350 degrees F and place the garlic and carrots on a baking tray, then drizzle with 1 tbsp of olive oil. Place in the oven to roast for approx. 15 minutes.

- While waiting, use a small knife or a vegetable peeler to peel down the cucumbers, then cut each cucumber into 2 to 3 inches slices long, depending on how deep you will like the cucumber cups to be.

- Use a teaspoon or a melon baller to scoop most of the flesh from each sliced cucumbers. Only leave a little at the bottom of the cup, enough to hold in the filling.

- Remove the garlic and carrot from the oven and put them into a food processor with the remaining ingredients plus the 2 tbsp of olive oil.

Blend on high speed for 2 to 3 minutes until you get a smooth consistency.

- Keep the hummus in the fridge to cool. Then use a tablespoon to dollop the hummus into the cucumber cups.
- Serve!

Pescatarian Diet Shopping List

You need a shopping list to have a complete meal plan. Here, I have assumed that you have some of the essentials, but this shopping list will be sufficient to make all the meals in the meal plan above and still have some leftovers to use for future meals. This list will be sufficient to feed up to 4 people.

Items	Quantity
Avocado	3
Almond milk	1 pint
Basil	1 small bunch
Broccoli	1
Blueberries	1 small punnet
Butter	2 sticks
Bread	1 small loaf

Cashew nuts	½ cup
Carrots	2 lbs
Butternut squash	1
Celery	5
Cauliflower	2
Chickpeas	3 tins
Cheddar	0.5 lbs
Chopped tomatoes	1 tin
Chocolate chips	6oz
Cucumber	2
Coconut milk	2 tins
Cilantro	1 small bunch
Garden peas	6oz
Galangal	3oz
Fresh fusilli paste	1 lb
Feta	0.5 lbs
Eggs	24
Honey	4oz
Green chili	2
Green beans	6OZ
Ginger	4oz
Garlic	4 bulbs

Macaroni fillet	1
Macaroni pasta	0.5 lbs
Lime	1
Lemon	3
Kidney bean	1 tin
Parmesan	5oz tub
Onion	1lbs
Mushrooms	0.5 lbs
Mixed peppers	0.5 lbs
Milk `	1 pint
Red chili	1
Raisins	4oz
Protein powder	4 tbsp
Pinto beans	1 tin
Peanut butter	4 tbsp
Parsley	4 tbsp
Shallots	4
Scallions	10
Sardines	0.5 lbs
Salmon	2 small fillets
Sweet potato	2

Spinach	8oz
Rolled oats	2 cups
Red lentils	1 cup
Tuna (tinned)	2
Tomatoes	4 lbs
Tilapia fillets	2
Teriyaki sauce	6oz
White potatoes	4
Udon noodles	6oz
Zucchini	1

Dinner Recipes

Grilled Tilapia with Lemon Butter, Capers and Orzo

Prep Time: 30 mins

Cook Time: 10 mins

Total Time: 40 mins

Serves 4

Ingredients

- Lemon (juiced) -2
- Lemon (finely zested) – 1
- Shallot (thinly sliced) - 1
- Heavy cream - 1 splash
- Olive oil - 3 tbsp

- Drained capers - ¼ cup
- Dry white wine - ½ cup
- Tilapia fillets – 4 (8 oz)
- Unsalted butter - 1 stick (cut into cubes)
- Flat-leaf parsley leaves (chopped) - ¼ cup
- Orzo, cooked al dente - ½ lb(s)
- Freshly ground black pepper
- Salt

Instructions

- Add the juice, lemon zest, shallot, and wine in a small saucepan and mix over high heat.
- Cook until the mixture reduces by half.
- Remove from heat and allow to cool
- Whisk the butter, cream and wine mixture together in a small bowl, then season with pepper and salt
- Cover with a lid and keep to refrigerate for approximately 30 minutes

- You can make the lemon butter a day before and keep in the refrigerator. Bring to room temperature before you serve
- Heat the grill to high
- Apply oil on both sides of the fish using a brush, then season the fish with pepper and salt
- Grill the fish for about three to four minutes on each side or until it turns light golden brown and slightly charred.
- Toss the orzo with two tablespoons of parsley and a few tablespoons of lemon butter. Season with pepper and salt
- Move the orzo to a platter
- Remove the fish from the grill, place the fillets on the orzo, then top each fillet with the capers and some lemon butter
- Use the remaining parsley to garnish your meal
- Serve!

Grilled Seafood Pasta Fra Diavolo

Prep Time: 25 Min

Total Time: 70 Min

Serves: 4 - 6

Ingredients

For Chili Oil

- Red chili flakes – 1 tablespoon
- Olive oil - ½ cup

For Spicy Tomato Sauce

- Kosher salt - ¼ tsp
- Anaheim chile pepper – 1 (halved and seeded)
- Campari tomatoes – 1 lb (halved)

For Seafood Pasta

- White wine - ½ cup
- Linguini - 1 lb(s)
- Lobster tails – 2
- Shallots – 2 (finely chopped)
- Kosher salt
- Garlic - 1 clove (finely chopped)
- Freshly ground black pepper
- Unsalted butter - 1 Tbsp
- Freshly grated parmesan - ¾ cup
- Freshly chopped parsley - 2 Tbsp
- Clams - 8 oz (scrubbed)
- Large Shrimp - 8 Oz (Shelled And Deveined)

- Zest of 2 lemons

Instruction

Chili Oil

- Combine the crushed red pepper flakes and the oil in a thick small saucepan. Boil over low heat for about five minutes or until a thermometer dipped into the oil shows 180°F

- Drain the oil into a heatproof container.

Spicy Tomato Sauce

- Get a large nonstick grill pan and heat over medium-high heat.

- Sprinkle salt on the chile and tomatoes then drizzle the chile and tomatoes with two teaspoons of the chili oil.

- Grill for approximately 4 minutes on each side, or until soft and charred. Then move the tomatoes into a bowl.

- Coarsely chop the chile before adding to the bowl that has the tomatoes.

Seafood Pasta

- Fill a large saucepan with salted water and bring to boil over medium-high heat. Once boiling, add the lobster tails and cook for about 4 minutes or until the meat is opaque and the shells turn red.

- Transfer the lobster tails to a cutting board, while the water remains on heat. Add the linguine to the boiling water and cook for about 6 minutes, until the pasta starts to soften but remains firm to bite. Stir occasionally. Reserve ¼ cup of the cooking water and drain the rest

- Get the seafood ready while the pasta is cooking. Cut through the top of the lobster shells, then cut each tail meat in half lengthwise. Move the sliced meat to a big bowl and then add the shrimp. Sprinkle 1 teaspoon of salt and 1 ½ tablespoons of the chili oil and toss to coat.

- Over medium-high heat, heat a big nonstick grill pan. Grill the shrimp and lobster tails for four minutes on each side until thoroughly cooked. Then transfer the shrimp to a big bowl. Chop the lobster into small pieces then mix with the shrimp.

- Place a big saucepan on medium-high heat, add 2 tablespoons of chili oil. Then add the garlic, ½ teaspoon salt, and shallots. Cook for about four minutes while occasionally stirring, until soft. Add the white wine and the spicy tomato sauce to the saucepan. Allow to boil.

- Add the clams to the saucepan and cook with the pan covered, for about four to six minutes, until the clams open

- Add the reserved cooking water, Parmesan, and the pasta to the pan. Toss to coat. Add in the lemon zest, butter, parsley, lemon zest, black pepper, and salt. Stir before you add the lobster and shrimp, then drizzle the remaining chili oil.

- Serve!

Cumin Grilled Sea Scallops with Red Pepper-Tahini Vinaigrette and Chickpea Salad

Prep Time: 20 mins

Cook Time: 26 mins

Total Time: 26 mins

Serves: 4 - 6

Ingredients

Scallops

- Large sea scallops - 20

- Ground cumin - 2 tsp

- Olive oil - 1 tbsp

- Black pepper - 1 tsp ground
- Kosher salt - 1 Tbsp

Chickpea Salad

- Olive oil - ¼ cup
- Fresh lemon juice - ¼ cup
- Ground cumin - 1 tbsp
- Kosher salt - 2 tsp
- Cayenne pepper - ½ tsp
- Freshly ground black pepper - ½ tsp
- Serrano peppers (grill, peel, deseed and thinly slice lengthwise) - 2
- Chickpeas, rinse and drain - 2 (16-oz) cans
- Large yellow bell pepper, grill, peel, seed and finely dice – 1
- Finely chopped chives - ¼ cup
- Finely chopped flat-leaf parsley - ¼ cup

Red Pepper-Tahini Vinaigrette

- Sherry vinegar - ¼ cup
- Red bell peppers (grill, peel, deseed and chop) - 2
- Saffron - 1 pinch
- Garlic, chopped - 2 cloves
- Olive oil - ½ cup

- Honey - 2 tbsp
- Tahini - 2 tbsp
- Kosher salt - ¼ tsp
- Freshly ground black pepper - ¼ cup
- Hot water - ¼ cup

Instructions

Scallops

- Heat your grill to high.
- Use a brush to oil the scallops on both sides
- Mix the pepper, salt and cumin in a small bowl then season each scallop with your mixture
- Grill the scallop for about two to three minutes on each side until golden brown and crusty.

Red Pepper-Tahini Vinaigrette

- Steep the saffron in a bowl of hot water for approximately five minutes to bloom.
- Then put the saffron mixture in your blender, add salt and pepper, tahini, garlic, honey, red pepper, and sherry. Blend until smooth. While blending, slowly sprinkle in the oil and continue to blend until well mixed.

- You can make the vinaigrette about 4 hours before use. Just keep covered and refrigerated. Allow it to cool to room temperature before you serve.

Chickpea Salad

- Beat together the cayenne, cumin, lemon juice, pepper, salt, and oil in a big bowl. Add the remaining ingredients then stir well.
- Move the salad into a big serving platter, cover with a lid, and allow to sit at room temperature for a minimum of 30 minutes and up to 2 hours before you serve.

Mackerel and Rhubarb Salad

SERVES 2

Ingredients

- Fennel - ½ bulb
- Rhubarb - 2 stalks
- Cider vinegar - 3 Tbsp
- Juice and zest of 1 orange
- Extra-virgin olive oil - 1 Tbsp
- Smoked mackerel fillets - 2

- Maple syrup - 2 Tbsp

- Watercress - 2 handfuls

- Freshly ground black pepper

- Walnuts - 2 Tbsp

Instructions

- Slice the fennel thinly with a mandolin and place it in a bowl.

- Pour the vinegar on the sliced fennel, then pour enough water to cover the fennel. Cover with plastic wrap and keep in the fridge for approximately one hour.

- Preheat your oven to 400 degrees F.

- Cut the pieces, about 2-inch sizes, then place on a baking sheet. Drizzle all of the maple syrup and three tablespoons of orange juice on the rhubarb. Mix thoroughly. Season with ground black pepper and put in the oven to roast for approximately 15 minutes.

- Drain the fennel then use a tea towel to pat dry. Flake the mackerel fillets then place it on a plate along with the walnuts, fennel, rhubarb, and watercress. Add one tablespoon of orange juice and the olive oil to a bowl, mix and drizzle over the salad.

- Sprinkle some black pepper and the orange zest. Serve!

Crispy Baked Salmon Fingers with Minty Peas

Prep Time: 10 minutes

Cook Time: 20 minutes

Total Time: 30 Minutes

Serves: 4

Ingredients

- Well-shaken buttermilk - 1 cup
- Light spelt/ unbleached all-purpose flour - 1/2 cup
- Cornmeal (either fine or medium-grain) - 1 cup
- Dried breadcrumbs ¬- 1 cup
- Salt, divided - 3/4 tsp
- Grapeseed oil - 1 tbsp
- Ground black pepper - 1/8 tsp
- Fresh shelled green peas or frozen peas - 3 cups (defrosted)
- Skinless salmon fillets - 4 (6 oz)

- Sliced fresh mint - 2 Tbsp

- Unsalted butter - 2 Tbsp

Directions

- Preheat oven to 400-degrees F.

- Place parchment paper on a large rimmed baking sheet.

- Pour the flour into a big bowl.

- Add the buttermilk to a large pie plate or glass baking dish.

- Mix ½ tsp salt and pepper, breadcrumbs, cornmeal, and oil in a large skillet. Toast over medium heat. Stir occasionally for about five minutes, until light brown. Transfer the cornmeal mixture to a separate large plate.

- Slice the salmon into 2-inch wide fingers. Taking each slice at a time, throw each fish finger into flour, shake off excess, soak in buttermilk and then coat each fish finger in the cornmeal mixture.

- Place on the baking sheet, tuck in any thin pieces of fish to give you uniform fingers. Repeat the steps above with the remaining flour, fish, cornmeal, and buttermilk mixture.

- Bake in the oven until fish flakes easily, and the crust is firm. This should take about 12 to 15 minutes.

- While the fish is baking, heat the peas and butter in a big skillet over medium heat for about two to four minutes, until hot and bright green.

- Stir in the remaining teaspoon of salt and the mint into the skillet.

- Use a regular metal spatula or a fish spatula to transfer the fish fingers to your serving dish along with the peas. Serve!

Oysters with Spicy Tomato Ice

SERVES 48

Ingredients

- San Marzano tomatoes (28-oz can) – 1

- Large oysters - 4 dozen

- White wine - 1 cup

- Seafood seasoning - 2 Tbsp

- Sugar - ½ cup

- Salt - 1 tsp

- Your preferred hot sauce - 1 Tbsp

- Lemons – 4 (juice and zest)

Instructions

- Prepare the granita one or two days before use. Squeeze and drain the liquid from the tomato into a small pot. Add sugar, wine, and spice and then cook on high heat while stirring continuously for about five minutes, until the liquid reduces by half.
- Pour the tomatoes into your blender, add the lemon juice and zest as well as the hot sauce. Add the spiced tomato juice and gently blend until smooth.
- Pour mixture into a pair of mason jars. Close loosely and put in the freezer. Hourly, tighten the lid, and shake the jars strongly until the mixture is frozen smooth. Keep in the fridge overnight. The ice can stay in the freezer for months so that you have it handy when next you want to enjoy a few oysters.
- When ready to consume, let the eaters carefully shuck the oysters while ensuring to keep all their fingers and liquor in the shell. Use the upside-

down tops to keep the oysters steady so as not to lose any drop of flavors.

- Scrape and place a spoonful of ice on each of the oysters. You can either serve the oysters one at a time or share all the oysters at once.

- Enjoy your meal whichever way you want.

Barbecued Mahi Mahi with Yellow Pepper-Cilantro Pesto

Prep Time: 15 Min

Total Time: 21 Min

SERVES: 4

Ingredients

Barbecue Rub

- Ancho chile powder - 1 Tbsp

- Spanish paprika - 2 Tbsp

- Ground cumin - 2 tsp

- Chile de arbol powder - 1 tsp

- Dark brown sugar - 2 tsp

- Coarsely ground black pepper - 1 tsp

- Kosher salt - 1 tsp

Yellow Pepper-Cilantro Pesto

- Garlic, chopped - 1 clove

- Extra-virgin olive oil - ½ cup

- Pine nuts - 2 tbsp

- Large yellow bell peppers (grill, peel, deseed and chop) - 2

- Chopped cilantro leaves - 1 cup

- Freshly grated pepper - 1 tsp

- grated parmesan - 3 tbsp

- Kosher salt - 1 tsp

Mahi-mahi

- Olive oil - 4 tsp

- Mahi-mahi fillets (8 oz each) - 4

- Cilantro leaves

- Barbecue rub

Instructions

Barbecue Rub

- Add all ingredients for the barbecue rub in a small bowl and mix.

Yellow Pepper-Cilantro Pesto

- Add the pine nuts, cheese, cilantro, garlic, and peppers in a food processor and mix until well combined. While the motor is still running, add the oil and blend until it is well mixed then season with the pepper and salt to taste.

Mahi-mahi

- Heat the grill to high.

- Use a brush to oil both sides of the fillet.

- Rub one side of each fillet with a tablespoon of the barbecue rub, then position them on the grill with the rubbed side facing down. Cook for about two to three minutes, until a crust has formed and the fillets are slightly charred.

- Now turn the fish to the other side and grill for another three to four minutes or until cooked to medium done.

- Garnish with cilantro leaves and top each of the fillets with tablespoons of the pesto.

Pan-Seared Salmon with Kale and Apple Salad

Prep Time: 20 Min

Total Time: 30 Min

Serves 4

Ingredients

- Fresh lemon juice - 3 Tbsp

- 5-oz center-cut salmon fillets – 4 (about 1-inch thick)
- Olive oil - 3 Tbsp
- Whole wheat dinner rolls - 4
- Kosher salt
- Dates - ¼ cup
- Kale, remove the ribs and slice the leaves very thinly – 1 bunch (about 6 cups)
- Honeycrisp apple – 1
- Toasted slivered almonds - 3 Tbsp
- Finely grated pecorino - ¼ cup
- Freshly ground black pepper

Instructions

- Allow the salmon to cool to room temperature ten minutes before cook time.
- While waiting, whisk together ¼ teaspoon of salt, the lemon juice, and two tablespoons of the olive oil in a large bowl before adding the kale. Throw lightly to coat, then keep aside for ten minutes.
- Cut the apple into matchsticks and the dates into thin slivers. Then add the almonds, cheese,

apples, and dates to the kale. Add pepper to taste, toss well and keep aside.

- Sprinkle pepper and ½ teaspoon of salt all over the salmon.

- Heat the remaining oil in a big nonstick pot over medium-low heat. Increase the heat to medium-high once the oil is hot.

- Place the salmon in the pan, with the skin side facing up. Cook for about four minutes, until golden brown on one side.

- Use a spatula to turn the fish to the other side and cook for another three minutes, until it feels firm to touch.

- Evenly divide the salad, salmons, and rolls into four plates

Salmon and Avocado Burger

Prep Time: 15 Min

Total Time: 25 Min

Serves 4

Ingredients

- Dill, chopped - 2 tbsp

- Fresh salmon, skin removed - 1 lb(s)

- Prepared horseradish - 2 tsp

- Dijon mustard - 1 tsp

- Egg white – 1

- Salt - ¼ tsp

- Whole wheat buns - 4

- Avocado, thinly sliced - ½

- Crème Fraiche or sour cream - ¼ cup

- Pea shoots - ½ cup

- Freshly ground pepper

Instructions

- Cut the salmon into pieces, about ¼-inch per piece, and put in a medium-sized bowl. Stir in the egg white, Dijon, horseradish, pepper, salt, and dill. Cover and allow to chill for approximately 30 minutes.

- Place a skillet over medium heat, then scoop ½ cup of the salmon mixture into the pan once hot. Gently press into a patty. Do the same with the remaining salmon mixture. Allow to cook for approximately 3 minutes or until the bottom turns golden.

- Flip to the other side and cook for another three minutes or until the patty sets.
- Place the salmon on a bun. Then top each burger with a tablespoon of crème Fraiche, pea shoots, and avocado slices.

Whitefish, Prawn and Vegetable Green Curry with Coconut Rice

Prep Time: 10 Min

Total Time: 45 Min

Serves 4 – 6

Ingredients

Green Curry Sauce

- Coriander seeds - 2 tsp
- Cumin seeds - 2 tsp
- Medium onion, sliced – 1
- Lemongrass, chopped - 1 stalk
- Garlic, sliced - 2 cloves
- Ginger, grated - 1 ½ inch piece
- Thai red chili, deseed and chop – 1

- Coconut milk (400 ml cans) - 2

- Small green peppers, core, and dice - 3

- Fish sauce - 4 tbsp

Coconut Rice

- jasmine rice - 1 cup

- salt - 1 pinch

- coconut oil - 2 tsp

- water - 1 ½ cups

To Plate

- Green pepper, diced – 1

- Vegetable oil - 2 tsp

- Red pepper, diced – 1

- Cauliflower, cut into florets - 1 small head

- White fish, cut into 1-inch pieces - ½ lb(s)

- Large oceanwise prawns, peel and devein - 12

- Lime wedges

- Salt, to taste

- Fresh coriander - ½ bunch

Instructions

Green Curry Sauce

- Place the coriander and cumin seeds into a frypan and gently heat for some minutes until they begin to get dark and sweet-smelling.
- Pour the seeds into a mortar and pestle or a grinder and grind until smooth.
- Sauté the lemongrass, chilis, ginger, garlic, onions, and ground spices until soft.
- Then add the fish sauce and coconut milk, bring to a simmer for about five minutes.
- Remove from heat. Transfer to a blender, add green peppers and puree in batches until smooth.
- Keep aside.

Coconut Rice

- Rinse the rice under cold running water until the water appears clear.
- Add water to a pot, add the rice and bring to a boil. Lower the heat to a simmer and cover pot.
- Cook for another 15 minutes
- Take away from heat and place the coconut oil on top.

To Plate

- Sauté the vegetables in a big pan until they start to soften, then add the fish and prawns and sauté for a few minutes more.

- Add the green curry sauce to the pan and heat for some seconds more.

- Serve with rice. Add your seasonings to taste and garnish with fresh coriander and some slices of limes.

Salad Niçoise with Smoked Trout and Dijon Lemon Dressing

Prep   Time: 40   minutes

Assembly   Time: 2   minutes

Serves: 4

Ingredients

- Smoked trout, chopped - 1 medium filet

- Niçoise olives - ½ cup

- Small potatoes, cook until tender - 1 lb.

- French green beans, trimmed and blanched - 2 cups

- Cherry tomatoes, halved - ½ pint

- Capers - 3 tbsp

- Hard-boiled eggs, halved - 4

- Radishes, thinly sliced - 4-5

- Boston lettuce leaves (rinse and dry)

- Salt-packed anchovies (optional) - 3-4

- Fresh dill, to taste

Dijon lemon dressing

- Olive oil - 1 cup

- Garlic - 1 clove

- Fresh lemon juice - 2 Tbsp

- Dijon mustard - 1 Tbsp

- Fresh cracked black pepper and Kosher salt, to taste

- Shallot, minced – 1

Instructions

- Mince the garlic on a chopping board and sprinkle with coarse salt. Use the flat side of a knife to press the salt and garlic together to give you a smooth paste.

- Transfer the mixture to a bowl and whisk in your lemon juice, pepper, salt, shallots, mustard, and oil. Keep aside.

- Place the butter lettuce at the bottom of a large bowl or a serving platter and then neatly line up your ingredients in rows.
- Drizzle with more pepper and salt (adjust to your taste) and the Dijon lemon dressing. Serve!

Lump Crab Cakes with Cocktail Remoulade Sauce

Prep Time: 110 Min

Total Time: 110 Min

SERVES 4

Ingredients

- Jumbo lump crabmeat, picked through for bits of shell - 1 lb(s)
- White sandwich bread, crusts removed - 4 slices
- Mayonnaise - ¼ cup
- Finely grated lemon zest - 2 tsp
- Baby spinach - 1 lb(s)
- Green onions, finely chopped – 2
- Worcestershire sauce - 1 tsp
- Hot sauce, like Tabasco - ¼ tsp
- Seafood seasoning, like Old Bay - 1 tsp

- Freshly ground black pepper and Kosher salt

- Unsalted butter - 5 Tbsp

- Large egg, lightly beaten – 1

- Garlic, thinly sliced - 1 small clove

- Lemon wedges, for serving

- Cocktail Remoulade, for serving, (recipes below)

Cocktail Remoulade

- Ketchup - ⅓ cup

- Mayonnaise - ⅓ cup

- Finely chopped flat-leaf parsley - 1 Tbsp

- Prepared horseradish - 2 Tbsp

- White wine vinegar - 1 Tbsp

- Whole grain mustard - 1 Tbsp

- Green onion, finely chopped – 1

- Finely chopped capers - 2 tsp

- Freshly ground black pepper and Kosher salt

Instructions

- Put the bread into a food processor and pulse to get coarse breadcrumbs. Transfer content to a big bowl.

- Add the lemon zest, green onions, Worcestershire, 1/4 teaspoon salt, hot sauce, seafood seasoning, mayonnaise, a few grinds of pepper, and crab to the bowl and mix gently. Then add the eggs and mix again.

- Pour the mixture into eight 3-inch wide crab cake cups and refrigerate for approximately 30 mins.

- Place a large nonstick skillet over medium heat and melt three tablespoons of butter. Cook the crab cakes for about four minutes on each side until heated through and golden brown on both sides.

- Move the cakes to a big plate and cover lightly with a foil.

- Add the remaining butter to a large pot and melt over medium heat. Then add garlic, cook and stir for about two minutes, until fragrant. Add the spinach, bit by bit, cook and toss until just wilted—season with pepper and salt.

- Share the spinach across four plates then top with the crab cakes. Serve with lemon wedges and Cocktail Remoulade

Cocktail Remoulade

- Mix the horseradish, green onion, ketchup, capers, mayonnaise, vinegar, mustard, parsley, pepper, and salt in a bowl.

- Cover with a lid and keep in the refrigerator for a minimum of 1 hour. The remoulade can stay refrigerated for up to 3 days.

Salad Niçoise and Tuna with Dijon Lemon Dressing

Prep Time: 40 minutes

Assembly Time: 2 minutes

Serves: 4

Ingredients

- Niçoise olives - ½ cup

- Small potatoes, cook until tender - 1 lb.

- Boston lettuce leaves (rinse and dry)

- Oil-packed tuna, drained - 1 jar

- French green beans, trimmed and blanched - 2 cups

- Cherry tomatoes, halved - ½ pint

- Capers - 3 tbsp

- Hard-boiled eggs, quartered - 4

- Radishes, thinly sliced - 4-5
- Salt-packed anchovies (optional) - 3-4
- Fresh dill, to taste

Dijon lemon dressing

- Olive oil - 1 cup
- Garlic - 1 clove
- Fresh lemon juice - 2 Tbsp
- Dijon mustard - 1 Tbsp
- Fresh cracked black pepper and Kosher salt, to taste
- Shallot, minced – 1

Instructions

- Mince the garlic on a chopping board and sprinkle with coarse salt. Use the flat side of a knife to press the salt and garlic together to create a smooth paste.
- Transfer the mixture to a bowl and whisk in the lemon juice, pepper, salt, shallots, mustard, and oil. Keep aside
- Place the butter lettuce at the bottom of a large bowl or on a serving platter and then neatly line up your ingredients in rows.

- Drizzle with more pepper and salt (according to your taste) and the Dijon lemon dressing. Serve!

Halibut Green Curry

Prep Time15 Min

Total Time 40 Min

Serves 4

Ingredients

- Packed fresh mint leaves - 1 cup
- Packed fresh cilantro leaves - 1 cup (plus more for garnish)
- Coconut milk - ⅓ cup
- Light brown sugar - 2 tsp
- Grapeseed oil - 2 Tbsp
- Juice of 1 lime, plus wedges for serving
- Garlic - 1 small clove
- Serrano pepper, seeded - ½
- Fresh ginger, peel, and chop - 1 (2-inch) piece
- Halibut, about 1/2-inch thick (skin removed) - 4 (6-oz) fillets
- Kosher salt

- Kale, stemmed, wash and tear into bite-size pieces - 1 large bunch

Instructions

- Preheat the oven to 350-degree F.

- Add one tablespoon of oil, two tablespoons of water, brown sugar, coconut milk, lime juice, mint, garlic, cilantro, ginger, 1/4 teaspoon salt, and pepper into a food processor. Blend until smooth, then move to a small bowl.

- Line a baking sheet with a 24-inch piece of foil. Toss the kale with a pinch of salt and the remaining tablespoon of oil. Place the kale in a single layer in the middle of the foil.

- Snuggle the fish filets on the kale, then sprinkle ¼ teaspoon of salt on it.

- Spread the green curry sauce evenly over each of the fillets.

- Loosely place another 24" of foil on top the fillets and seal the edges (try not to let the foil touch the fish.

- Bake in the oven for about 15 to 20 minutes, until the fish is well cooked, and the greens are crisp-tender.

- Gently remove the foil and share the greens and the fish into four plates.
- Use the cilantro as toppings and serve with lime wedges.

Dungeness Crab Tacos with Radish Sprouts

Prep Time20 Min

Total Time 30 Min

Serves 2

Ingredients

Tacos

- Zest and Juice of 1 lemon, divided
- Dijon mustard - 2 Tbsp
- Miso paste - 2 Tbsp
- Honey (or maple syrup) - 2 Tbsp
- Canola oil - 1 cup
- Ripe avocado – 1
- Fresh cooked Ocean Wise Dungeness crab - ¾ cup
- Freshly ground pepper and Sea salt
- Crispy wonton shells - 6

For Serving

- Radish sprouts - ½ cup

- Radishes - ½ cup (thinly shaved)

Instructions

Tacos

- Reserve one teaspoon of lemon juice. Mix the remaining lemon juice with canola oil, miso paste, honey, mustard, and lemon zest in a blender to prepare the dressing.

- Use a fork to mash the avocado and season with pepper, salt, and one teaspoon of lemon juice.

- Mix about ¼ cup of the dressing with the Ocean Wise crab meat. Adjust as needed. Store the remaining dressing in the refrigerator for up to two weeks.

To serve

- Stuff the wonton shells with the crab-meat mixture. Scoop the avocado mixture into a plate then position the assembled tacos on top. Garnish using sprouts and radish slices.

Olive Oil Poached Tuna

Serves 4

Ingredients

Warm Chickpea Salad

- Red onion, diced - ½ of small
- Roasted Garlic - 3 clove
- 540 ml canned Chickpeas - 1
- Torn basil - 5 leaves
- Grape tomatoes - 1 cup (halved)
- Lemon juice and zest - ½
- Olive oil - ¼ cup
- Salt and pepper to taste
- Chicken stock - ½ cup

For Olive and Herb Dressing

- Total fresh herbs (parsley, green onions, chives), chopped - ¾ cup
- Celery, sliced very thinly on diagonal, reserving leaves - 1 inner stalk
- One lemon juice and zest
- Chopped pitted black olives - 3 tbsp
- Olive oil - 3 tbsp
- Salt and pepper

For Tuna

- Olive oil - 4 ½ cups

- 5-oz Very fresh tuna steaks - 4
- Garlic - 1 clove
- Whole black peppercorn - 2 tbsp
- Bay leaves – 2
- Rosemary - 1 sprig
- Salt and pepper

Balsamic Glaze

- Balsamic vinegar - 1 cup
- Honey - 2 Tbsp

Tuna Tartare (Chef's Treat)

- Capers (rinse, drain and finely chop) - 1 tsp
- Sushi grade tuna, diced - 4 oz
- Extra virgin olive oil - 1 tbsp
- Lemon juice - 1 tsp
- Green onion, finely chopped - 1 tsp
- Dijon mustard - ½ tsp
- Salt and pepper to taste
- endive – 1
- Extra virgin olive oil (if desired) - 1 tsp

Instructions

Warm Chick Pea Salad

- Heat 1 tablespoon of olive oil in a sauté pan.

- Sauté the red onion and roasted garlic for about 1 minute, then add the chickpeas and toss.

- Roughly mash garlic in the pot and one-third of the chickpeas

- Increase the heat to high and add the chicken stock. Allow simmering while reducing the heat slightly.

- Remove from heat and toss in the lemon juice, basil, tomatoes, and lemon zest.

- Dress with three tablespoons of infused poaching oil.

- Add salt and pepper. Keep aside.

For Herb and Olive Dressing

- Toss all the ingredients for the herbs and olive salad together, add salt and pepper to taste. Keep aside at room temperature.

For Tuna

- Get your poaching oil ready: in a medium thick-bottomed pot, add the peppercorns, rosemary, bay leaves, garlic, and olive oil.

- Allow to simmer then remove from heat. Keep to stand overnight.

- Use a thermometer to get the poaching oil up to 130 degrees F in a medium thick-bottomed pot.

- Get the tuna out of the fridge and keep in room temperature for a minimum of 10 minutes.

- Season both sides of the tuna with pepper and salt.

- Once you confirm that the oil has reached 130 degrees F, slowly place the tuna steaks into the oil. Keep the tuna in the oil for approx. seven to eight minutes, add one or two more minutes for a thicker steak.

Balsamic Glaze

- Mix the honey and balsamic vinegar in a small pot. Reduce to low heat until you get a syrup consistency.

Tuna Tartare (Chef's Treat)

- Combine all ingredients for tartare into a ceramic bowl or small glass.

- Season with pepper and salt to taste.

- Then add an extra teaspoon of olive oil if you want.
- To serve, tear the leaves off the endive and use the endive to scoop up tartare.

Grilled Salmon Steaks

Prep time: 20 min

Total time: 30 min

Serves 4

Ingredients

- Whole cumin seed - 1 tsp
- Salmon steaks (1-inch thick) - 4
- Whole coriander seed - 1 tsp
- Whole fennel seed - ½ tsp
- Dry green peppercorns - 1 tsp
- Olive or canola oil to coat steaks
- Kosher salt or Sea salt

Instructions

- Get your grill ready by turning gas grill to medium-high or lighting four quarts of charcoal.

- Check that the steaks do not have pin bones by rubbing your fingers over the surface of the meat. Remove all pin bones with pliers and bone tweezers made for culinary uses.

- Use a sharp boning or paring knife to trim the bones from the cavity side of the meat.

- Trim the stomach flaps in such a way that one side will be missing about 1 inch of meat while the other side about 2 inches of skin.

- Roll up the skinless part into the hollow of the cavity, then wrap the other part around the outside to give you a shape like a filet mignon. Use two passes of butcher's twine to tie in place. Ensure it is not too tight to prevent the fish from popping out while cooking.

- Add the peppercorns, fennel, coriander, and cumin on a double-thick piece of aluminum. Toast over the grill, shake gently until the seeds give this sweet smell.

- Pour seeds into a pepper grinder or grind in mortar and pestle.

- Lightly apply oil on the steak, add salt to season, then generously apply the ground seeds on each side of the steaks.

- Use a towel or rag dipped in a little canola oil to quickly wipe hot grill grate, then grill the fish for about three minutes for each side, until fish is barely translucent at the center and well colored on the outside.

- Serve!

Lobster Stew

SERVES 4

Ingredients

- Chopped fresh chervil - 1 tbsp

- Butter - 3 tbsp

- Lobsters, about 675 g each – 2

- Onion, chopped – 1

- Tomato paste - 1 tbsp

- Asparagus tips - 12

- Cognac - 2 tbsp

- Yellow zucchini - 12 slices

- Shelled peas - ¼ cup

- Radishes – 6 (halved)

- Lemon juice, to taste

- Salt and pepper - 1 pinch

Instructions

- Fill a big pot with water and bring to a boil. Add the lobsters to the pot with the head first and steam for approximately 4 minutes.

- Drain the water and rinse the lobster under cold water until its cool to touch.

- Remove the shell from the lobsters, wrap the meat, and keep in the refrigerator until you are ready to use it. (you should have two tails and four claws intact. You can cut them into halves lengthwise.)

- Reserve the shells and 12 lobster legs but discard the body. Put the shells into your food processor and chop them into pieces or use a mallet.

- Take half of the butter and heat in a large sauté pan, add the onions and cook until soft. Add the tomato paste, stir, then add the lobster shells.

- Pour over the Cognac and flame.

- Once the flame dies down, pour 750 ml or 3 cups of water and cook until the liquid reduces to 1 and a half cups.

- Strain the liquid, press down on the shell to remove all the liquid. Pour the extracted liquid back to the sauté pan.

- While waiting for the sauce to reduce, steam the vegetables in a separate pot of boiling salted water for about 30 seconds to 2 minutes. The time varies depending on the veggies you are using.

- When each is done, use a slotted spoon to lift the veggies to a strainer and immediately dip into an ice bath to maintain the color.

- Allow the lobster stock in the sauté pan to simmer without covering the pot. Then add the lobster and poach slowly for approximately three minutes.

- Add the veggies and cook for another two minutes.

- Arrange a whole claw and half a tail in each of the four soup bowls.

- Evenly share the veggies around the meat

- You should have 4 cups of sauce per dish. If you get more, boil it down, then whisk in the remaining butter at the end.

- Season with lemon juice, pepper, and salt (adjust to your taste.)

- Ladle over the veggies and the lobster, scatter over chervil.

- Serve!

Grilled Tuna Tataki Bowl

Prep Time: 60 Min

Total Time: 80 Min

Serves 2

Ingredients

Bowl

- Soy sauce - ¼ cup

- Fresh sushi-grade yellowfin tuna steak - 1 lb(s)

- Toasted sesame oil - 3 Tbsp

- Toasted white or black sesame seeds - 1 heaping tsp

- Montreal steak Seasoning - 2 Tbsp

- ¼ seedless cucumber - thinly sliced
- Red radish - thinly sliced – 4
- Cilantro – chopped - ½ cup

Lime Chili Soy Sauce

- Garlic (finely minced) - 1 clove
- Light soy sauce - ¼ cup
- Ginger (finely minced) - 1 inch
- Chili oil - 1 tsp
- Freshly ground black pepper - ¼ tsp
- Lime (juiced) – 1

Instructions

Bowl

- Rinse the tuna steak under clean water and pat dry with paper towels.
- Place the steaks in a baking dish and add the sesame oil and soy sauce. Sprinkle each side of the steak with steak spice, ensure that both sides are well coated.
- Put in the refrigerator to marinate for about one to two hours.

- Once the steak has marinated, preheat your BBQ grill until it gets so hot that you can not place your hand over it for more than five seconds.

- Put the tuna on the grill without moving it for approx. four minutes.

- Then flip the tuna steak to the other side and grill for another two to three minutes. Confirm that both sides are well seared.

- Once the tuna is ready, move it to a tray and cover it with an aluminum foil. Keep aside for ten minutes.

- Cut the tuna steak, against the grain, then add to your bowl of fresh sticky rice, shallots, cilantro, cucumber, and raw radish.

- Dress with spoonfuls of sauce as you like.

Lime Chili Soy Sauce

- To get the sauce ready, add ginger, garlic, chili oil, Soy sauce, pepper, and lime juice in a small box. Mix thoroughly and set aside.

Fish Mappas

Prep Time: 15 MINS

Cook Time: 20 MINS

Serves 4

Ingredients

- Skinless, boneless pollock fillets – 4, cut into 1 ½ inch chunks (you can also go for other sustainable white fish)
- Sunflower or vegetable oil - 1 tbsp
- Basmati rice - 300g
- Large onion – 2 (sliced)
- Tomatoes - 450g (cut into chunks)
- Garlic cloves – 2 (chopped)
- Tikka curry paste - 3 tbsp
- Coriander - ½ small pack (roughly chopped)
- Coconut milk - 400g can

Instructions

- Boil water in a large saucepan and cook the rice according to the instruction on the pack.
- Heat the oil in a big, wide pot over medium heat. Add onions and cook for about five to ten minutes, until the onions turn soft and begin to color.

- Add the tomatoes and garlic and fry for two minutes. Then add the curry paste and fry for another two minutes. Pour in the coconut milk and allow to boil.

- Add the fish to the wide pot and simmer gently for about five to eight minutes, until well cooked. Take off heat.

- Sprinkle the coriander over the curry and serve with the cooked rice.

Fish Tacos

Prep Time: 15 MINS

Cook Time: 15 MINS

Makes 4

Ingredients

- Chipotle paste or harissa - 1 tsp

- Lemon sole goujons - 220g pack

- Mayonnaise - 6 tbsp

- White cabbage, finely shredded - 175g

- Soft corn tortillas – 4

- Small red onion, finely sliced or chopped – 1

- Chopped coriander - a good handful
- Juice of 1 small lime
- Plus wedges to serve (optional)

Instructions

- Heat your oven to 390 degrees F. Place the goujons on a baking sheet, making sure there is enough space between each one. Bake for about 12 to 15 minutes or as directed on the pack, until crispy.
- Mix the harissa or chipotle with the mayonnaise.
- Warm the tortillas (best way to do this is over a gas flame).
- Next, get the salad ready: Toss the onion, coriander, and cabbage with some salt and lime juice.
- Spread the tortillas with little of the spiced mayonnaise, then place the fish and the salad down the center.
- Add a little more mayonnaise as a topping, then fold and devour with your fingers.
- You can serve with lime wedges if you want.

Falafel Burgers

PREP TIME: 10 MINS

COOK TIME: 6 MINS

SERVES 4

Ingredients

- Curly parsley or flat-leaf parsley – a handful
- Chickpea - 400g can (rinse and drain)
- Small red onion – 1 (roughly chop)
- Ground cumin - 1 tsp
- Garlic– 1 clove (chopped)
- Ground coriander - 1 tsp
- Chili powder or harissa paste – ½ tsp
- Sunflower oil - 2 tbsp
- Plain flour - 2 tbsp

To Serve

- Toasted pitta bread
- Green salad
- Tomato salsa - 200g tub

Instructions

- Drain the chickpeas and pat dry using kitchen paper.

- Add the chickpeas to a food processor, then add one garlic clove, 1 tsp ground coriander, 2 tbsp plain flour, one small roughly chopped red onion, ½ tsp of chili powder or harissa paste, 1 tsp ground cumin, a handful of flat-leaf parsley, and a little salt.
- Blend until you get a fairly smooth texture then use your hands to shape into four patties.
- Heat two tablespoons of sunflower oil in a non-stick frypan, add the burgers and fry for approx. 3 minutes on each side, or until lightly golden.
- Serve with the green salad, 200g tub tomato salsa, and the toasted pitta bread.

The Easy Fish Pie Recipe

Prep Time: 15 MINS

Cook Time: 45 MINS

Makes 6-8 Toddler Meals/ Serves a Family of 4 to 6

Ingredients

- Fish pie mix – 1 x pack/ 400g (salmon, cod, smoked haddock, etc.)
- Maris Piper potatoes – 1 kg (peel and halve)

- Butter – 25g (plus 2 tbsp)

- Milk - 400ml (plus a splash)

- Plain flour - 25g

- Spring onions – 4 (finely sliced)

- Chives - ½ a 25g pack or a small bunch (finely snipped)

- Dijon or English mustard - 1 tsp

- Frozen sweetcorn – a handful

- Grated cheddar – a handful

- Frozen petits pois – a handful

Instructions

- Heat your oven to 390 degrees F.

- Peel and halve the potatoes then place in a saucepan with enough water to cover the potatoes. Leave to boil, then simmer until tender.

- Once cooked, drain the water and mash the potatoes with two tablespoons of butter and a splash of milk – Season with the ground black pepper.

- In another pan, add four finely sliced spring onions, 25g plain flour, and 25g butter then heat gently for about 1 to 2 mins, until the butter melts, stirring occasionally.

- Slowly whisk in 400 ml of milk using a balloon whisk if you own one. Allow to boil while stirring to avoid it sticking to the bottom of the pan and forming lumps. Cook for about three to four minutes until you get a thick texture.

- Put off the heat and stir in a small bunch of finely snipped chives, a handful of sweetcorn, 1 tsp Dijon or English mustard, a handful of petits pois and 320g-400g mixed fish.

- Spoon the mixture into 6 to 8 ramekins or an ovenproof dish.

- Spoon the potato on top of the mixture, then sprinkle a handful of the grated cheddar cheese.

- Place in the oven for about twenty to 25 minutes or until it begins to bubble at the edges and turn golden.

- Alternatively, cover and place the mini pies or the pies in the fridge to use for another meal.

Coconut Fish Curry

Prep time: 15 mins

Cook time: 15 mins

Serves 4

Ingredients

- Skinless hake fillets - 450g (cut into rectangles)

- Vegetable oil - 1 tbsp

- Ginger - thumb-sized piece (finely grated)

- Onion – 1 (finely chopped)

- Garlic – 3 cloves (crushed)

- Shrimp paste - 1 tsp

- Lemongrass – 2 stalks (split and bruise with a rolling pin)

- Small red chili – 1 (shred and remove the seeds if you do not like it too hot)

- Medium curry powder - 1 heaped tbsp

- Muscovado sugar - 1 heaped tbsp light

- Coconut milk - 400g can

- Coriander - small bunch (stems finely chopped)

- Lime – 1 (halved)

- Frozen raw whole prawns - 220g pack

- Cooked rice, to serve

Instructions

- Heat 1 tablespoon of oil in a wide, lidded fry pan, add the onion, and cook for approx. 5 mins until soft. Increase the heat a little and then stir in the lemongrass, shrimp paste, garlic, ginger and chili, cook for another two minutes.

- Add the sugar and curry powder and continue to stir.

- Once the sugar begins to melt, and the content of the frypan starts to clump together, add two tablespoons of water, coconut milk, and the coriander stems, then bring to a simmer.

- Now add the fish to the frypan, tuck in the prawns, then squeeze over half of the lime.

- Cover with the lid and allow to simmer for another five minutes until the fish is cooked and the prawns appear pink.

- Check that the seasoning suits your taste and add a little more lime to the sauce if you want.

- Scatter the sauce over the coriander leaves and serve with cooked rice.

Creamy Courgette Lasagne

Prep time: 10 mins

Cook time: 20 mins

Serves 4

Ingredients

- Dried lasagne sheets – 9
- Onion- 1 (finely chopped)
- Sunflower oil - 1 tbsp
- Tomato sauce - 350g jar (for pasta)
- 700g Courgetti – about 6 (coarsely grated)
- Garlic– 2 cloves (crushed)
- Cheddar – 50g
- Ricotta – 250g

Instructions

- Heat your oven to 390 degrees F.
- Boil a pot of water and then add the lasagne sheets to cook for approx. five minutes until softened but not too cooked.
- Rinse under cold water then sprinkle a little oil to prevent them from sticking together.
- Heat your oil in a large frypan, add the onions and fry for 3 minutes, then add the garlic and

courgettes and fry until the courgetti turns bright green and soft.

- Stir in 2/3 of both the cheddar and the ricotta, then add season to taste.

- Heat the tomato sauce for two minutes in the microwave on High until hot.

- Layer up the lasagne in a large baking dish, beginning with half the courgetti mix, followed by the pasta then the tomato sauce. Repeat the steps then top with blobs of the leftover ricotta. Now scatter the rest of the cheddar on top.

- Place on the top shelf of your oven and bake for approx. 10 minutes until the cheese is golden and the pasta is tender.

Shepherd's Pie Filling

Prep time: 10 mins

Cook time: 50 mins - 1 hr

Serves 4

Ingredients

- 1 lb Very big carrots – 2 (cut into sugar-cube sizes)
- Olive oil – 1 tbsp

- Large onion – 1 (halve and slice)

- Thyme - 2 tbsp (chopped)

- Red wine - 200ml

- Sweet potatoes – 950g (peel and cut into chunks)

- Chopped tomatoes - 400g can

- Vegetable stock cubes – 2

- Vegetarian mature cheddar - 85g (grated)

- Green lentils - 410g can

- Butter – 25g

Instructions

- Heat one tablespoon of olive oil in a frypan, add the sliced onion to the pot and fry until golden.

- Add the chopped carrots and most of the chopped thyme. Reserve a little of the thyme for sprinkling.

- Pour in the chopped tomatoes, 150ml water, 200ml red wine, crush the vegetable stock cubes, turn the mixture and simmer for ten minutes.

- Add the green lentils with its juice, then cover and simmer for additional 10 minutes until the lentils are pulpy. The carrots should also be bite-able.

- In another pot, boil the diced sweet potatoes for approx. 15 minutes until tender. Then drain the liquid, and mash with seasonings and butter to taste.

- Heap the lentil mixture into your pie dish, scoop the potato mash on top, then sprinkle the remaining thyme and all of the vegetarian mature cheddar. You can cover and keep in the fridge for two days or freeze for up to a month.

- If cooking straight away, heat your oven to 370 degrees F and cook for approx. 20 minutes or for 40 minutes if chilled, until hot and golden.

- Serve with broccoli.

Simple Fish Stew

Prep time: 10 mins

Cook time: 20 mins - 25 mins

Serves 2

Ingredients

- Chopped tomatoes - 400g can

- Olive oil - 1 tbsp

- Raw shelled king prawns - 85g

- Fennel seeds – 1 tsp

- Hot fish stock - 500ml (heated to a simmer)

- Carrots – 2 (diced)

- Garlic – 2 cloves (finely chopped)

- Celery – 2 sticks (diced)

- Leeks – 2 (thinly sliced)

- Skinless pollock fillets - 2 (about 200g), thaw if frozen, and cut into chunks

Instructions

- Add the oil to a large pan and heat. Then add the garlic, celery, carrots, and fennel seeds. Cook for five minutes until the veggies begin to soften.

- Tip in the fish stock, tomatoes, and leeks, season and allow to boil, then cover with a lid and simmer for about 15 to 20 minutes, until the sauce has thickened and the veggies are tender.

- Add the fish to the pot, toss the prawns and cook for another 2 minutes until lightly cooked.

- Transfer to a bowl and serve with a spoon.

Baked Sea Bass With Lemon Caper Dressing

Prep time: 10 mins

Cook time: 10 mins

Serves 4

Ingredients

- Sea bass fillets - 4oz

- Olive oil

For Caper Dressing

- Gluten-free Dijon mustard - 2 tsp

- Zest 1 lemon – 1 (grated)

- Extra virgin olive oil - 3 tbsp

- Small caper - 2 tbsp

- Lemon juice - 2 tbsp

- Chopped flat-leaf parsley - 2 tbsp, plus a few extra leaves (optional)

Instructions

- Make the dressing by mixing the oil with the mustard, 1 tbsp water, capers, some seasoning, lemon zest, and juice. Do not add the parsley at this time except if you are serving immediately, as the acid in the lemon will make the color of the veggie disappear if you leave them together for a long time.

- Heat your oven to 430 degrees F.

- Place parchment paper on your baking tray, then put the fish on top with the skin-side facing up.

- Brush the fish skin with oil and sprinkle some flaky salt on it.

- Keep in the oven to bake for approx. 7 minutes or until the flesh flakes when you test with a knife.

- Transfer the fish to warm serving plates, spoon the dressings on it and then scatter some more parsley leaves if you want.

Sesame Salmon, Sweet Potato Mash & Purple Sprouting Broccoli

Prep time: 10 mins

Cook time: 15 mins

Serves 2

Ingredients

- Low-salt soy sauce - 1 tbsp

- Sesame oil - 1 ½ tbsp

- Garlic – 1 clove (crushed)

- Ginger - thumb-sized piece (grated)
- Honey – 1 tsp
- Lime – 1 (cut into wedges)
- Sweet potatoes – 2 (scrub and cut into wedges)
- Boneless skinless salmon fillets – 2 (250g)
- Red chili, thinly sliced – 1 (deseed if you do not like it too hot)
- Sesame seeds - 1 tbsp

Instructions

- Heat the oven to 390 degrees F. Place parchment paper on a baking tray.
- Mix the honey, garlic, ginger, soy, and ½ tbsp of sesame oil.
- Add all the sweet potatoes and the lime wedges into a glass bowl.
- Cover with cling film and microwave on high speed for about 12 to 14 minutes, until totally soft.
- Spread the salmon and the broccoli out on the baking tray.
- Spread the marinade on the contents of the baking tray and season.

- Place in the oven to roast for about 10 to 12 minutes, then sprinkle the sesame seeds on top.

- Take out the lime wedges then use a fork to mash the sweet potato roughly.

- Add the remaining sesame oil, some seasoning, and the chili then mix.

- Serve!

Honey & Orange Roast Sea Bass With Lentils

Prep time: 15 mins

Cook time: 10 mins

Serves 2

Ingredients

- Large skin-on sea bass fillets – 2

- Zest and juice of ½ orange

- Clear honey - 2 tsp

- Wholegrain mustard - 2 tsp

- Olive oil - 2 tbsp

- Ready-to-eat puy lentils - 250g pouch

- Watercress - 100g

- Parsley – small bunch (chopped)

- Dill – small bunch (chopped)

Ingredients

- Heat oven to 390 degrees F.
- Place each of the sea bass fillets on individual squares of foil, with the skin-side facing down.
- Mix together 1 tbsp olive oil, mustard, some seasoning, honey, and orange zest and drizzle it over the sea bass fillets.
- Pull up the sides of the foil and twist the edges together to create separate parcels.
- Place all the parcels on the prepared baking tray and place in the oven to bake for approx. 10 minutes, until it flakes easily when pressed with a knife (this shows that the fish is well cooked).
- Follow the instructions on the lentils pack to warm the lentils, then mix with the remaining oil, the watercress, orange juice, seasoning, and herbs.
- Share the lentils between two plates, then top each plate with a sea bass fillet.
- Drizzle any remaining roasting juices caught in the foil, then serve!

Hearty Pasta Soup

Prep time: 5 mins

Cook time: 25 mins

Serves 4

Ingredients

- Carrots – 2 (chopped)
- Olive oil - 1 tbsp
- Large onion – 1 (finely chopped)
- Vegetable stock – 5 cups
- Frozen mixed pea and beans - 200g
- Chopped tomato - 400g can
- Freshly filled tortellini - 250g pack (you can use ricotta and spinach)
- Parmesan to serve (grated)
- Basil leaves – a handful (optional)

Instructions

- Heat oil in a frypan, add the onions and carrots and fry for 5 minutes until it begins to soften.

- Add the tomatoes and veggie stock and simmer for 10 minutes. Then add the beans and peas and cook for another 5 minutes.
- Stir in the pasta once the veggie is tender. Allow to boil then simmer for 2 minutes, until the pasta is well cooked.
- If using basil, stir it in now. Season.
- Serve in bowls and sprinkle the parmesan and slices of garlic bread as the topping.

Butternut Squash & Sage Risotto

Prep time: 10 mins

Cook time: 40 mins

Serves 4

Ingredients

- Butternut squash - 1kg (peel and cut into bite-size chunks)
- Sage – a bunch (leaves picked, roughly chop half and leave half whole)
- Olive oil - 3 tbsp
- Vegetable stock – 6 cups
- Butter - 50g

- Risotto rice – 300g

- Onion – 1 (finely chopped)

- Parmesan, finely grated – 50g (or any vegetable of your choice)

- White wine - 1 small glass

Instructions

- Before you go ahead to make the risotto, first heat the oven to 430 degrees F. Toss the chopped sage and the squash in 1 tablespoon of oil then spread them into a shallow roasting tin and place in the oven to roast for approx. 30 minutes until soft and brown.

- Now go ahead to prepare the risotto while the squash is in the oven. Once the stock boils, reduce heat to low to simmer.

- In another pan, over medium heat, melt half of the butter, then stir in the onions and cook for about 8 to 10 minutes, stirring occasionally, until soft but not colored.

- Now add the rice to the onions and stir until the rice is completely coated in butter. Continue to stir until the rice becomes shiny and the edges start to appear transparent.

- Pour the wine to the pan and simmer until it becomes totally evaporated. Now add the stock, one spoon at a time and stir the rice over low heat for about 25 to 30 minutes, until the rice is cooked firm to the bite (al dente). The risotto should be slightly soupy and creamy.

- At the same time, lightly fry all the whole sage leaves in a little olive oil until it turns crisp. Keep aside on a kitchen paper.

- Once the squash is cooked, leave half whole and mash the remaining half to a rough puree texture.

- When the risotto is just cooked, stir in the pureed squash, then add butter and cheese and allow to rest for a few minutes.

- Scatter the risotto on the serving dish with the crisp sage leaves and the whole chunks of squash.

Thai-Style Steamed Fish

Prep time: 10 mins - 15 mins

Cook time: 15 mins

Serves 2

Ingredients

- Trout fillets weighing about 5 oz each – 2
- Garlic – 1 small clove (chopped)
- Fresh ginger root – a small knob (peel and chop)
- Small red chili – 1 (seeded and finely chopped)
- Zest and juice of 1 lime - grated
- Soy sauce - 2 tbsp
- Baby pak choi – 3 (each quartered lengthways)

Instructions

- Place the fish fillets beside each other on a large square foil, scatter the lime zest, garlic, ginger, and chili over them.
- Drizzle the lime juice on top of the fish fillets, then spread the pieces of pak choi on top and by the sides of the fish.
- Now pour the soy sauce on top of the pak choi and seal the foil loosely to make a package. Ensure to leave enough space at the top so that the steam can circulate as the fish cooks.
- Steam for approx. 15 minutes.

- If you do not have a steamer, place the parcel on a heatproof bowl and place over a pan of gently simmering water. Cover with a lid and allow to steam.
- Serve!

Fish pie - in four steps

Prep time: 45 mins

Cook time: 30 mins

Serves 4

Ingredients

- Skinless smoked haddock fillet - 400g
- Skinless white fish fillet - 400g
- Full-fat milk - 600ml
- Cloves – 4
- Small onion – 1 (quartered)
- Bay leaves – 2
- Parsley – a small bunch, leaves only (chopped)
- Eggs – 4
- Butter – 100g
- Plain flour - 50g
- Cheddar – 50g (grated)
- Freshly grated nutmeg – a pinch

- Floury potato – 1kg (peel and cut into even-sized chunks)

Instructions

- Poach the skinless smoked haddock fillets and white fish fillets. Put the fish in the frypan and pour 500ml of the full-fat milk into the frypan. Quarter the onion and stud each of the onion with a clove. Add to the frypan along with two bay leaves. Allow the milk to boil; you will see small bubbles appear. Now reduce the heat and simmer for approx. 8 minutes.
- Transfer the fish to a plate and strain the milk to a jug to cool. Flake the fishes into big pieces in the baking tray.
- **Hard boil the eggs.** Add water to a small pan and bring to a gentle boil, then add the eggs using a slotted spoon. Cook the eggs for exactly 8 minutes, then drain and place the eggs in a bowl of cold water. Once cool, peel, slice, and place on top of the fish.
- Chop some of the parsley leaves and scatter over the fish.

- **Get your sauce ready**. Melt the butter in a pan, then add the plain four, stir and cook over moderate heat for 1 minute. Remove from heat, pour a little of the cold poaching milk, stir till well blended. Keep adding more milk slowly until you get a smooth sauce. Return pan to heat, allow to boil, and cook for about 5 minutes while stirring often until it coats the back of your spoon.

- Take away from heat. Season with a pinch of freshly grated nutmeg, pepper, and salt, then pour over the fish.

- **Assemble and bake**—Preheat oven to 390 degrees F. Boil the already cut floury potatoes for 20 minutes. Drain the liquid, season and mash with the 100ml full-fat milk and 50g butter remaining. Use the mixture to top your pie - begin from the edge of the dish and work your way in. Seal the edges by pushing the mash to the right of the edges. Use a fork to fluff the top, then sprinkle the grated cheddar, now place in the oven to bake for approx. 30 minutes.

Spinach, Sweet Potato & Lentil Dhal

Prep time: 10 mins

Cook time: 35 mins

Serves 4

Ingredients

- Red onion – 1 (finely chopped)
- Sesame oil - 1 tbsp
- Garlic – 1 clove (crushed)
- Ginger - thumb-sized piece (peel and chop finely)
- Red chili – 1 (finely chopped)
- Ground cumin - 1 ½ tsp
- Spinach - 80g bag
- Ground turmeric - 1 ½ tsp
- Red split lentils - 250g
- Sweet potatoes – 2 (cut into even chunks)
- Vegetable stock - 600ml
- Thai basil, to serve - ½ small pack (leaves torn)
- Spring onions, to serve– 4 (sliced on the diagonal)

Instructions

- Heat one tablespoon of sesame oil in a wide pan that has a tight-fitting lid.

- Add the chopped red onion and cook on low heat for about ten minutes, stirring regularly, until softened.

- Add the chopped red chili, crushed garlic clove, and chopped ginger, cook for one minute before you add 1 ½ tsp ground cumin, and 1 ½ tsp ground turmeric—Cook for another one minute.

- Increase the heat to medium, then add the chopped sweet potatoes and stir all the contents together so that the sweet potato gets well coated in the mixture.

- Add some seasoning, the vegetable stock, and the red split lentils to the pot.

- Allow the liquid to boil, then lower the heat, cover the pot, and allow it to cook for approx. twenty minutes until the potato is barely holding its shape, and the lentils are tender.

- Taste and add more seasoning if required, then slowly stir in the spinach. Once the spinach wilts, top up with the torn basil leaves and the sliced spring onion to serve.

- Alternatively, allow the content to cool totally, then share it into airtight containers and place in the fridge to eat when ready.

Gnocchi & Tomato Bake

Prep time: 5 mins

Cook time: 25 mins

Total time: 30 mins

Serves 4

Ingredients

- Olive oil - 1 tbsp

- Onion- 1 (chopped)

- Garlic – 1 clove (crushed)

- Red pepper – 1 (deseed and finely chop)

- Chopped tomatoes - 400g can

- Gnocchi - 500g pack

- Mozzarella - half a 125g ball (torn into chunks)

- Basil – a handful (leaves torn)

Ingredients

- Set the grill to high heat.
- Heat 1 tablespoon of olive oil in a large frypan, add the chopped onions and red pepper and cook for 5 minutes until softened.
- Stir in the crushed garlic clove and fry for a minute, then add the gnocchi and the tomatoes. Bring it to a simmer. Let it bubble for about ten to fifteen minutes while you stir regularly until the sauce thickens and the gnocchi is soft.
- Season, stir in some of the torn basil leaves, then move to a big ovenproof dish.
- Scatter the torn mozzarella ball and then grill for about 5 to 6 minutes until the cheese is golden and bubbling.
- Ready!

Salmon & leek parcel

Prep time: 10 mins

Cook time: 20 mins Plus Chiling

Serves 2

Ingredients

- Skinless salmon fillets – 2

- Leek, thinly sliced - 250g (about 3 small ones)

- Baby potatoes

- Mascarpone - 85g

- Chopped dill - 1 tbsp

- Chopped dill – 1 tsp

- A good squeeze of lemon juice

- Lemon – ½, grated zest of ¼,

- Capers - 2-3 tsp

- Wilted spinach, to serve

Instructions

- Heat oven to 390 degrees F. Place two sheets of parchment paper on your work surface. It should be big enough to wrap up each of the salmon fillets.

- Fill a pot with six tablespoons of water, add the leeks, and bring to boil. Cook for about 5 minutes, until the leeks are almost tender and the water is almost gone. Stir in some seasoning, one tablespoon of dill, and the mascarpone.

- Scoop out half of the creamy leeks into the center of one of the parchment papers, then place a salmon fillet on top of it. Repeat the same for the second parchment sheet. Squeeze some lemon juice on it with a sprinkle of the lemon zest, then spread the remaining teaspoon of dill and the capers over the salmon fillets.

- Bring up the parchment paper above the fish and fold the edges over the fish several times. Do the same with the ends of the sheet, then place on a baking sheet. Ensure to space the two parcels.
- Place in the oven to bake for about 12 to 15 minutes, depending on how soft you like your fish.
- Once done, gently tear open the sheet. Serve with lemon wedges, wilted spinach, and baby potatoes, if you like.

Steamed Trout With Mint & Dill Dressing

Prep time: 10 mins

Cook time: 25 mins

Serves 2

Ingredients

- New potatoes – 120g (halved)
- Asparagus spears - 170g pack (woody ends trimmed
- Vegetable bouillon powder made up to 225ml with water - 1½ tsp
- Frozen peas - 80g
- Fine green beans - 80g (trimmed)
- Skinless trout fillets – 2
- Lemon – 2 slices

For the Dressing

- English mustard powder - ¼ tsp
- Bio yogurt - 4 tbsp
- Chopped dill - 2 tsp
- Cider vinegar - 1 tsp
- Finely chopped mint – 1 tsp

Instructions

- Place the potatoes in a pan of boiling water and simmer until tender.
- Chop the asparagus into half to shorten the spears, then slice the ends without the tips. Add the bouillon into a large non-stick pan, then add

- the beans and asparagus, cover and cook for about 5 minutes.

- Add the peas to the cooking pot and top with the lemon slices and the trout. Cover and cook for an additional 5 minutes until the fish gets flaky but still juicy.

- In another bowl, mix the vinegar, yogurt, dill, mustard powder, and mint. Stir in two to three tablespoons of the fish cooking juice.

- Dish the veggies and any remaining juice into serving bowls, top with the herb and fish dressing, then serve with the potatoes.

Satay Sweet Potato Curry

Prep time: 15 mins

Cook time: 45 mins

Serves 4

Ingredients

- Sweet potato - 500g (peeled and cut into chunks)
- Coconut oil - 1 tbsp

- Thai red curry paste (read the label to confirm it's vegetarian/ vegan) - 3 tbsp
- Onion – 1 (chopped)
- Ginger - thumb-sized piece (grated)
- Garlic – 2 cloves (grated)
- Coconut milk - 400ml can
- Spinach – 200g bag
- Smooth peanut butter - 1 tbsp
- Lime – 1 (juiced)
- Dry roasted peanuts, to serve
- Cooked rice, to serve

Instructions

- Melt one tablespoon of coconut oil in a cooking pan over medium heat, then add chopped onion and cook for about 5 minutes, until softened. Add the grated ginger and garlic cloves and cook for another 1 minute until you can perceive the fragrance.
- Stir in the smooth peanut butter, 200 ml of water, 400ml of coconut milk, the peeled and chopped sweet potatoes as well as the Thai red curry paste.

- Allow to boil, then lower the heat and simmer uncovered for 25 to 30 minutes or until the sweet potato turns soft.

- Add the spinach, stir, add the juice of 1 lime, stir, then add your seasons.

- Serve with cooked rice, sprinkle some dry roasted peanuts if you like.

Mushroom & spinach risotto

Prep time: 50 - 55 mins

Serves 2

Ingredients

- Olive oil -1 tbsp

- Butter – 25g

- Onion – 1 (chopped)

- Chestnut mushrooms - 140g (sliced)

- Fat garlic – 1 clove (crushed)

- Arborio rice - 140g

- Dry white wine - 150ml

- Sundried tomatoes – 4 (chopped)

- Hot vegetable stock - 500ml

- Chopped fresh parsley – 2 tbsp

- Parmesan – 25g (freshly grated)

- Fresh young leaf spinach - 100g (washed if necessary)

- Green salad and warm ciabatta, to serve

Instructions

- Heat the butter and oil in a large frypan. Add the onion and cook for about 5 minutes until softened. Stir in the garlic and mushrooms and cook gently for another 2 to 3 minutes.

- Add the rice and stir to coat with the mushroom and onion mixture. Now add the wine and cook over medium heat for about 3 minutes, occasionally stirring, until the wine is fully absorbed.

- Lower the heat, add 125ml of veggie stock and the tomatoes, and cook until the liquid is absorbed, approx. 5 minutes. Pour another 125ml of the veggie stock and cook until fully absorbed. Repeat this until you have exhausted the stock, and the rice is tender and creamy.

- Now stir in half the parmesan and the parsley—season to taste. Spread the spinach over the risotto. Cover with lid and cook gently for about four to five minutes, until the spinach is just wilted.

- Serve and sprinkle the remaining parmesan on your dish.

Mediterranean Fish Gratins

Prep time: 25 mins

Cook time: 55 mins

Serves 6

Ingredients

- Large onion- 1 (thinly sliced)

- Olive oil - 3 tbsp

- Garlic – 3 large cloves (finely sliced)

- Fennel bulb – 1 (trimmed and thinly sliced)

- White wine – 150ml

- Coriander seeds - 1 heaped tsp (lightly crushed

- Tomato purée - 2 tbsp

- Chopped tomatoes with herbs - 2 x 400g cans

- A good pinch of saffron

- Bay leaf – 1

- Flat-leaf parsley - 1 small bunch (leaves roughly chopped)

- Fresh lemon juice - 1 tbsp

- Raw peeled king prawn - 350g

- Mixed skinless fish fillets - 900g (cut into chunks)

- Coarse dried breadcrumbs or panko – 50g

- Finely grated parmesan – 75g

- Green salad, to serve (optional)

Ingredients

- Heat the oil in a sauté pan or a large non-stick saucepan. Add the garlic, fennel coriander seeds, and onions to the pan and fry for 15 minutes, stirring regularly until the veggies are lightly colored and softened. Pour the wine to the pot, add the saffron, tomato purée, bay leaf, and tomatoes. Season and bring to a gentle simmer. Cook for another 15 minutes until thick, stirring occasionally.

- Heat the oven to 430 degrees F. add most of the parsley and the lemon juice into the tomato mixture, pop the raw prawns and fish pieces on top, stir well and cover tightly with a lid.

- Simmer over medium heat for about 4 to 5 minutes, or until the fish is almost done. Stir as the fish cooks, but be careful not to break up the fish.

- Scoop out the fish and hot tomato mixture into 6 different pie dishes. Each dish should hold about 350ml. Add the breadcrumbs, a little ground black pepper, the remaining parsley, and the cheese in a small bowl, mix then sprinkle on top of each pie dish.

- Place the dish on a baking tray and place in the oven to bake for approx. 20 minutes or until the pies become bubbly and golden brown.

- Serve with green salad, if desired.

Fish Tagine With Saffron & Almonds

Prep time: 15 mins

Cook time: 25 mins

Serves 4

Ingredients

- Large onion- 1 (chopped)
- Olive oil - 1 tbsp
- A good pinch of saffron
- Hot chicken or fish stock - 600ml
- Garlic – 2 cloves (crushed)
- Ginger - thumb-sized piece (peeled and grated)
- Cinnamon - 1 tsp
- Cherry tomatoes – 10 (halved)
- Green Chili - ½, finely sliced (deseeded if you don't like it too hot)
- Ground cumin - 2 tsp
- Tomato purée - 1 tbsp
- Ground coriander - 1 tsp
- Ground almond - 2 tbsp
- Zest 1 orange
- Juice of ½ orange
- Honey - 1 tbsp
- Coriander – small bunch (chopped)
- Whitefish - 700g (cut into large chunks)

- A handful of flaked almond, toasted
- Another ½ green Chili, to serve
- Natural yogurt, to serve
- Couscous

Instruction

- Heat oil in a large pot. Add the onion and cook until soft.
- Dip the saffron in the hot chicken or fish stock and leave to steep.
- Add the chili, ginger, and garlic to the pot and cook for another few minutes.
- Add the tomato purée and the spices, stir for some minutes until fragrant, then add the orange juice and zest, ground almonds, honey, saffron-scented stock, and the tomatoes, ensure to use all the saffron strands. Leave uncovered and cook for about 10 minutes, until the sauce has thickened a little and the tomatoes have broken down.
- Add the fish to the pot, check that the pieces are close to each other under the sauce. Cover the pot and simmer for 2 to 3 minutes on low heat, until just cooked. Check that you are satisfied

with the seasoning, scatter the toasted almonds, and add the coriander.

- Dish out and serve with the chili, blob of natural yogurt, and some couscous, if you like.

Fish pie fillets

Prep time: 10 mins

Cook time: 10 mins

Serves 4

Ingredients

- Thick white fish fillets – 4 x 6oz
- Half-fat soft cheese - 100g
- Dill, leaves only - small bunch (chopped)
- Frozen prawn - 200g (raw/ cooked, defrosted)
- Filo pastry - 4 sheets
- Parmesan – 1 tbsp (finely grated)

- Sunflower oil – 2 tsp

Instructions

- Heat your oven to 430 degrees F. Place the fish in a non-stick baking sheet and rub your seasoning all over. Mix the soft cheese and the dill in a small bowl, then stir in the prawns, be careful not to break them up. Season with ground black pepper, then evenly spread over the fish.

- Rub oil on the filo sheets then cut into thick strips. Squeeze the pastry up a little then crumple on top of the fish.

- Scatter parmesan on it and place in the oven to bake for 10 minutes until the pastry is golden and crisp and the fish is well cooked. If you used raw prawns, now is the time to check that they are well cooked.

- Serve with your salad or green beans.

Hot & Sour Fish Soup

PREP TIME: 15 MINS

COOK TIME: 30 MINS

EASY

SERVES 4

Ingredients

- Coriander seeds - 1 tsp
- Galangal or ginger – small piece (sliced)
- Fish or chicken stock – 850ml
- Thin rice noodles - 175g
- Fish sauce - 2 tbsp
- Fat red Chilies – 2 (deseeded and thinly sliced)
- Garlic - 3 cloves (thinly sliced)
- Raw, tail-on tiger prawns - 300g
- Skinless salmon fillet – 7oz (cut into small cubes)
- Spring onions – 4 (chopped)
- Handful mint leaves (torn)
- A handful of coriander leaves
- Juice of 2 limes

Instructions

- Put the ginger/ galangal and the coriander seeds in a saucepan. Add the fish or chicken stock, allow to boil, then simmer gently for about 5 minutes. Set aside to stand for approx. 10 minutes.

- Cook the noodles according to the instruction on the pack. Drain the water and keep warm.
- Return the stock to heat. Once boiled, add the garlic, chilies, and fish sauce, lower the heat and allow to simmer for two minutes.
- Now add the salmon and prawns, return to simmer, and cook gently for 5 minutes or until the salmon and prawns are well cooked and firm. Add the lime juice, herbs, and spring onions to taste.
- Share the noodles into soup bowls, use a slotted spoon to lift the fish and prawns then place on top the noodles. Season the hot stock and pour it into the different bowls.
- Serve with spring rolls by the side.

Prawn Katsu Burgers

Prep time: 30 mins

Cook time: 10 mins

Serves 2

Ingredients

- Vegetable oil or sunflower oil, for frying

- Brioche burger buns – 2

For the burgers

- Spring onion – 1 (sliced)

- Egg white – ½

- Raw peeled prawns – 200g

- Cornflour - 1 tbsp

- Panko breadcrumbs - 100g

For the slaw

- Juice ½ lemon

- White cabbage – ¼ (finely shredded)

- Mayonnaise - 1 tbsp

For the Chili mayo

- Mayonnaise - 3 tbsp

- Sweet Chili sauce or sriracha Chili sauce - 1 tbsp

Instructions

- To prepare the burgers, rinse the prawns under cold water, then use kitchen paper to pat dry. Tip the spring onion and half of the prawns into a food processor, add enough salt and pulse till you get a rough paste.

- Add the cornflour and the egg white, pulse a little more, then add the remaining prawns and pulse again to get them properly mixed.

- Add the breadcrumbs on a plate or a shallow dish. Use your hands to scoop out half of the prawn mixture and make a burger shape with the mixture. Now press the burger into the bread crumbs, flip to the other side and ensure that the burger is completely coated with the breadcrumbs. Do this for all the mixtures and crumbs, then arrange the burgers on a plate, cover with cling film and keep aside until you are ready to cook.

- Now mix all the ingredients for the chili mayo in a bowl. Also, add all the ingredients for the slaw in another bowl, season, then combine by tossing the plate. You can make the chill mayo, slaw, and burgers a day before and keep in the fridge.

- Time to cook the burgers. Add 2cm of oil in a frypan and heat until just about to simmer. Drop a breadcrumb into the oil; if it turns brown and sizzles, it means that the oil is starting to simmer. Gently fry the burgers for about 4 minutes on each side until it turns crispy and golden. You may need to turn them a couple of times to get them well cooked. Gently bring out the burger from the oil and place on kitchen paper to drain the oil.

- Cut the buns into two equal sizes and toast the cut sides under your grill.

- Gather the burgers together by spooning the slaw over the bottom of each of the bun, add a burger then top with the mayo

- Serve right away with extra chili mayo if you wish.

Cauliflower Cheese

Prep time: 10 mins

Cook time: 35 mins

Serves 6

Ingredients

- Large cauliflower – 1 (cut off leaves and break into pieces)

- Milk – 500ml

- Flour – 4 tbsp

- Butter – 50g

- Strong cheddar – 100g (grated)
- Breadcrumbs - 2-3 tbsp (if available)

Instructions

- Add water to a large saucepan and bring to a boil, then add the broken cauliflower and cook for about 5 minutes. Lift a piece to check that it is cooked.
- Once cooked, drain the liquid then place the cauliflower into an ovenproof dish.
- Heat your oven to 430 degrees F.
- Return the saucepan to heat and add the flour, butter, and milk.
- Whisk fast as the butter melts and the mixture begins to boil. You will no longer see the flour and the sauce will start to get thick. Whisk for another 2 minutes while the sauce gets nice and thick.
- Take off heat, stir in most of the cheddar cheese, and the cauliflower. Scatter the remaining cheese and three tablespoons of breadcrumbs.
- Place in the oven to bake for approx. 20 minutes until bubbling.

Burnt Aubergine Veggie Chili

Prep time: 25 mins

Cook time: 2 hrs

Serves 4

Ingredients

- Aubergine – 1
- Rapeseed oil or olive oil – 1 tbsp
- Red onion – 1 (diced)
- Carrots – 2 (finely diced)
- Green lentils or puy lentils - 70g (rinsed)
- Red lentils - 30g (rinsed)
- Kidney beans – 400g can
- Dark soy sauce - 3 tbsp
- Chopped tomatoes - 400g can
- Dark chocolate – 20g (finely chopped)
- Dried oregano - 2 tsp
- Vegetable stock - 800ml
- Chili powder - ¼ tsp
- Ground cumin - 2 tsp
- Sweet smoked paprika - 2 tsp
- Cinnamon - 1 tsp

- Coriander - 1 tsp
- Lime – ½ (juiced)

To serve

- Mashed avocado, tortilla chips, grated cheddar, sour cream or yogurt, roughly chopped coriander (optional)
- Brown rice

Instructions

- If you have a gas hob at home, place the aubergine directly on a lit ring to burn completely, using your kitchen tongs to turn occasionally until all the sides are burnt. You can also use a barbecue or set the grill to heat on the highest settings and cook the aubergine, turn at intervals until totally blackened (you may not get that same smoky flavor with the grill). Place on a plate and keep aside to cool, then peel out the burnt skin and remove the stem. Chop the flesh roughly and keep aside.
- Heat the oil in a large pan, then add the carrots, onions, and a pinch of salt. Fry for 15 to 20 minutes on low to medium heat until the carrots have softened.

- Now add all the lentils, soy sauce, the aubergine, chili powder, the spices, oregano, the kidney beans along with the liquid from the can, chocolates, and tomatoes. Stir well, then add the stock. Allow to boil, then reduce the heat to very low. Cover the pan with its lid and cook for about one and a half hours, checking and stirring every 20 minutes to prevent it from burning.

- Take off the lid and allow the mixture to simmer for about 15 minutes, over low to medium heat, until you get a thick sauce. Stir occasionally, then stir in the lime juice, taste and add more salt if needed.

- Serve hot with rice and any other accompaniments of your choice.

Mushroom Risotto

Prep time: 5 mins

Cook time: 25 mins (plus soaking)

Serves 4

Ingredients

- Dried porcini mushrooms - 50g

- Vegetable stock cube – 1

- Olive oil - 2 tbsp

- Onion – 1 (finely chopped)

- Garlic - 2 cloves (finely chopped)

- Chestnut mushrooms - 250g pack (chopped)

- Risotto rice, like arborio– 300g

- Butter – 25g

- White wine - 1 x 175ml glass

- Parsley leaves – a handful (chopped)

- Grana Padano or parmesan – 50g (freshly grated)

Instructions

- Add the dried porcini mushrooms to a large bowl, then pour 1 liter of boiling water into the bowl. Soak for approx. 20 minutes. Now, drain the liquid into another bowl, crush one vegetable stock cube into the liquid, then gently squeeze the mushrooms to remove the remaining liquid.

- Heat two tablespoons of olive oil in a deep frypan or shallow saucepan over medium heat. Add the chopped garlic and onions, then fry until soft. This should take about five minutes.

- Add the dried mushrooms and the chopped chestnut mushrooms, stir, add your pepper and salt. Cook for another 8 minutes until the fresh mushrooms get soft.

- Add the risotto rice to the pan and cook for 1 minute. Now add the white wine and allow to bubble until the liquid evaporates.

- Retain the pan on medium heat, add a quarter of the mushroom stock to the pan. Stir occasionally while the rice simmers, until all the liquid is absorbed. Then add the same amount of mushroom stock to the pot, stir and allow to simmer. By now, the content of the pan will become tender, plump, and creamy. Add the remaining stock to the pan. By this time, the rice should be almost cooked. Stir often until the rice is cooked. Add a little more water if the rice is still undercooked.

- Remove the pan from heat, add a handful of the chopped parsley leaves, the butter, half of the grated Grana Padano cheese, or parmesan to the pan.

- Cover the pan and keep aside for a few minutes while the rice takes up any excess liquid from the pot.

- Stir the risotto for the last time before you dish into your serving bowls, then scatter the remaining chopped parsley leaves and grated cheese before you serve.

Herb & Garlic Baked Cod with Romesco Sauce & Spinach

Prep time: 10 mins

Cook time: 20 mins

Serves 2

Ingredients

- Skinless cod - 2 x 140g (loin or pollock fillets)
- Baby spinach - 100g (wilt in the microwave or a pan)
- Rapeseed oil – 1 tbsp
- Rapeseed oil – 2 tsp
- Fresh thyme leaves - 1 tsp

- Large red pepper – 1 (sliced)

- Lemon – ½ (zested and juiced)

- Leeks – 2 (wash well and slice thinly)

- Garlic – 1 clove (finely grated)

- Vegetable bouillon powder - ¼ tsp

- Flaked almonds - 2 tbsp

- Tomato purée - 1 tbsp

- Apple cider vinegar - 1 tsp

Instructions

- Heat the oven to 430 degrees F and add the fish fillets into a shallow ovenproof dish so they can nestle in a single layer.

- Mix the garlic, thyme, and one tablespoon of rapeseed oil in a small bowl, then spoon over the fish. Now grate the lemon zest and add to the dish.

- Place in the oven to bake for about 10 to 12 minutes, until the fish flakes easily when tested.

- Now heat the remaining oil in a non-stick pan, add the leeks and pepper and fry for 5 minutes until soft. Then add the almonds and cook for another 5 minutes.

- Add five tablespoons of water, the apple cider vinegar, the tomato puree, and the bouillon powder and cook briefly to get the mixture warm.

- Now add the juice of half a lemon and blitz using a stick blender until you have a thick, pesto-like sauce.

- Serve with the wilted spinach and the fish.

Harissa Roast Salmon With Lemon Chickpea Couscous

Prep time: 30 mins

Cook time: 50 mins

Serves 8 - 10

Ingredients

For the salmon

- Large onions - 2 (halve and slice thinly)
- Olive oil - 2 tbsp

- Large fennel bulb – 1 (halve and slice thinly)

- Garlic – 1 clove (chopped)

- Cumin seeds - 1 tsp

- Lemon, zest – 1

- Harissa - 2 tbsp

- 4 oz boneless sides of salmon – 2 (skin removed)

- Agave nectar or clear honey - 1 tbsp

For the couscous

- Couscous – 300g

- Vegetable stock cube – 1

- Harissa - 2-3 tsp

- 2 x 400g cans chickpeas – 2 (drained)

- Currants - 50g

- Lemons – 2 (juiced)

- Lemon, zest – 1

- Olive oil - 2 tbsp

- A big bunch of flat-leaf parsley, chopped

- Toasted flaked almonds - 50g

- Lemon wedges, to serve

- Small bunch of mint - chopped (optional)

Instructions

- Heat 2 tbsp of oil in a large non-stick frypan, add the cumin seeds, garlic, fennel, and onions. Fry for about 15 minutes, occasionally stirring, until the vegetables are golden and soft. Now stir in the lemon zest and season. Keep aside to cool.

- Mix the harissa and the honey or agave. Place a salmon fillet, on a large sheet of baking parchment, with the skinned side facing down, then spread half of the harissa mixture on the salmon. Top evenly with the veggies, and cover with the other salmon fillet. Position it in a way that the thickest end of the fillet will be on top of the thinnest end. You can do these steps up to this point a day before, covered, and chilled.

- Heat your oven to 390 degrees F and place a large baking sheet into the oven. Apply the rest of the harissa mixture on the salmon, then lift the salmon with the parchment sheet and place on the hot baking sheet in the oven. Allow to bake for 30 minutes. Take out of the oven and confirm that the fish is well cooked all over. If not cooked as you like, return to the oven for another 5 minutes, then check again.

- Get your couscous ready. Crush the stock cube into a big bowl and add the couscous, currants, and harissa. Add two tablespoons of oil, your seasoning, lemon juice, and chickpeas into another bowl.

- Before you serve, pour 450ml of boiling water over the couscous, stir thoroughly, then cover with a plate and allow to soak for approx. 5 minutes. Now add the mint, parsley, and lemon zest to the bowl containing the chickpeas and stir thoroughly, then add the flaked almonds and the hot couscous.

- Serve with the salmon on a warm, big platter.

- The best way to move the salmon is to lift it with the parchment sheet, then slide it on top, with the lemon wedges by its side.

- To serve, you can either cut the salmon in slices or cut the salmon into thicker slices then halve to give chunky squares.

Salmon with Beetroot, Feta & Lime Salsa

Prep time: 10 mins

Cook time: 10 mins

Serves 2

Ingredients

- Skin-on salmon – 2 fillets
- Feta - 70g
- Cooked beetroot - 200g
- Limes – 2

Instructions

- Chop the feta and beetroot into small cubes then mix with the zest and juice of one lime and some seasoning. Then season the salmon fillets.
- Heat 2 tablespoons of oil in a non-stick frypan over high heat.
- When the oil is hot, add the salmon, with the skin-side facing down and cook for 3 minutes. Flip to the other side, lower the heat and cook for another four to five minutes.
- Cut the remaining lime into wedges.
- Serve your salmon with the lime wedges and the beetroot salsa.

Lentil & Sweet Potato Curry

Prep time: 10 mins

Cook time: 25 mins

Serves 2

Ingredients

- Olive or vegetable - 2 tbsp
- Red onion – 1 (chopped)
- Mustard seeds (any color) - 1 tsp
- Cumin seeds - 1 tsp
- Medium curry powder - 1 tbsp
- Green or red lentil (or a mixture) – 100g
- Medium sweet potatoes – 2 (peel and cut into chunks)
- Chopped tomato - 400g can
- Vegetable stock - 500ml
- Chickpea - 400g can (drained)
- Naan bread and natural yogurt, to serve
- ¼ small pack coriander (optional)

Instructions

- Heat two tablespoons of olive or vegetable oil in a large frypan, add the chopped red onion and cook until soft.
- Add the curry powder, mustard seeds and cumin seeds, cook for another one minute, then stir in the lentils, chopped tomatoes, vegetable stock, and the cut sweet tomatoes.
- Allow to boil, then cover and simmer for approx. 20 minutes until the sweet potatoes and the lentils are tender. Now add the drained chickpeas and heat through.
- Season to your taste, sprinkle the coriander, and serve with the naan bread and seasoned yogurt.

Lentil Ragu

Prep time: 15 mins

Cook time: 1 hr, 15 mins

Serves 6

Ingredients

- Olive oil - 3 tbsp
- Carrots – 3 (finely chopped)
- Onions – 2 (finely chopped)
- Celery – 3 sticks (finely chopped)
- Garlic – 3 cloves (crushed)
- Dried red lentils - 500g bag
- Tomato purée - 2 tbsp
- 400g cans chopped tomatoes - 2
- Dried oregano - 2 tsp
- Thyme - 2 tsp
- Vegetable stock – 4 ½ cups
- Bay leaves – 3
- Spaghetti - 500g
- Vegetarian or parmesan cheese, to serve (grated)

Instructions

- Heat the oil in a big saucepan, then add the garlic, celery, carrots, and onion. Cook gently for about 15 to 20 minutes until all the contents of the pot get soft. Now stir in the lentils, vegetable stock, herbs, tomato purée, and chopped tomatoes. Allow to simmer, then cook for another 40 to 50 minutes until the lentils are saucy and tender. Add a little more water if needed. Season.

- If you are eating immediately, reduce the heat while you cook the spaghetti according to the instruction on the pack. Then drain the water from the spaghetti, divide between pasta plates or bowls, spoon the sauce on top of the pasta then grate over some cheese.

- If not eating immediately, allow the sauce to cool then store in the fridge for up to 3 days or in the refrigerator for up to 3 months. To use, defrost portions night before at room temperature, then reheat gently before serving.

Next level fish pie

Prep Time: 40 Mins

Cook Time: 1 Hour

Serves 6

Ingredients

- Butter - 150g
- 400g shell-on raw prawns (peel and reserve the heads and the shells)
- Shallot – 1 (finely chopped)
- Smoked haddock – 400g (skin and trim [reserve these], dice flesh into large chunks)
- bay leaf – 1
- One vegetable stock cube or 1 tsp of vegetable bouillon powder
- Star anise – 1
- White wine – 150ml
- Whole milk – 5 cups
- Plain flour - 60g
- Low fat crème Fraiche - 200ml
- Skinless whitefish fillet - 400g (diced into large chunks)
- Salmon fillet – 200g (diced into large chunks)
- Capers - 2 tbsp (drain and finely chop)
- Lemon – 1 (juiced)
- King Edward potatoes - 1½ kg
- Medium cheddar or gruyere

- Ready salted crisps - 40g pack

- Spinach, watercress or peas, to serve

- Small splash Pernod (optional)

- Eggs – 4 (optional)

Instructions

- Heat 25g of butter in a shallow pot and sizzle the shallot for approx. 2 minutes. Now add smoked haddock skin and trimmings, the prawn shells and head, increase the heat and cook for about 5 minutes, until they begin to brown. Add the star anise and bay to the pot, then splash the Pernod and the wine. Stir and boil until the liquid evaporates, then pour 4 cups of milk and sprinkle in the vegetable bouillon. Allow the content of the pot to simmer for 15 minutes, turn off the heat. Use a potato masher to crush the shells and strain into a jug.

- Clean out the pot, melt another 60g of butter, then stir in the flour till you have a sandy paste. Cook on low heat for 2 minutes. Slowly stir in the flavored milk and the crème Fraiche. Simmer gently to get a very thick sauce—season to your taste. Take off heat and gently fold through all the prawns and fish, lemon juice, and capers. Scrape mixture into a large buttered baking dish.

- Preheat your oven to 430 degrees F. Add the potatoes to a large pot of water and bring to boil, then add your eggs and simmer for approx. 8 minutes. Take out the eggs from the pot, put in a bowl of cold water for some minutes before you peel, halve, and push into the prepared sauce.

- Drain the water from the potatoes, then mash with the remaining butter and milk. Pipe or spread the mash over the pie. Crush and/ or sprinkle the gruyere.

- Place the pie on a baking tray and put it in the oven to cook for approx. 35 minutes until it turns golden and just bubbly.

- Allow to sit for a minimum of 10 minutes before you eat with buttered watercress, peas, or spinach.

Roasted Vegetable Lasagne

Prep Time: 25 Mins

Cook Time: 1 Hr, 10 Mins

Serves 6

Ingredients

- Aubergines – 2
- Red peppers – 3
- Olive oil - 8 tbsp (plus a little for greasing)
- Fresh pack lasagne sheets - 300g
- Tomato sauce - ½ quantity (see below)
- White sauce - ½ quantity (see below)
- Cherry tomatoes – a handful (halved)
- Mozzarella - 125g ball (or vegetarian alternative)

Instructions

- Heat oven to 430 degrees F. Deseed, halve and cut the peppers into large chunks. Cut off the ends of the aubergines, then chop into about ½cm thick slices. Lightly oil two large baking pans, then place the aubergines and peppers on top. Add the olive oil and mix well, then place in the oven to roast for approx. 25 minutes, until lightly browned.

- Reduce the oven to 356 degrees F. Lightly grease an ovenproof serving dish. Spread the vegetables on the bottom of the serving dish, then pour over a third of the tomato sauce into the dish. Add a layer of lasagne on top, then sprinkle some of the white sauce. Repeat the steps until you have three layers of pasta.

- Now use your spoon to spread the remaining white sauce over the pasta, ensure that the whole surface is covered. Spread the mozzarella over the top with the tomatoes.
- Place in the oven to bake for another 45 minutes until golden and bubbling.
- Serve!

Energy, and Cleanse Your Body with the Alkaline
Diet. https://amzn.to/3aPZrSX

- LOW CALORIES DIET PLAN: Foods to Eat to Lose
  Weight and Stay Healthy. Includes 1,200 to 1,700-
  Calorie Meal Plans https://amzn.to/37vVyk1

- THE DIVERTICULITIS GUIDE TO LIVE PAIN-FREE:
  Diverticulitis Diet Plan, Foods to Eat & Avoid,
  Diagnosis and Tips for Causes, Recovery and
  Prevention https://amzn.to/38HTu8U